London I...... ....
Life & Music . . .

SHANE MacGOWAN

London Irish Punk
Life & Music . . .
SHANE MacGOWAN

Joe Merrick

OMNIBUS PRESS
LONDON · NEW YORK · SYDNEY

Cover designed by Phil Gambril
Picture research by Nikki Lloyd

ISBN: 0.7119.7653.8
Order No: OP 48136

Exclusive Distributors:
Music Sales Limited,
8/9 Frith Street,
London W1D 3JB, UK.

Music Sales Corporation,
257 Park Avenue South,
New York, NY 10010, USA.

The Five Mile Press,
22 Summit Road,
Noble Park,
Victoria 3174, Australia.

To the Music Trade only:
Music Sales Limited,
8/9 Frith Street,
London W1D 3JB, UK.

Printed in Great Britain by MPG Books Ltd, Bodmin.
Typeset by Galleon Typesetting, Ipswich.

A catalogue record for this book is available from the British Library.

www.omnibuspress.com

CONTENTS

Acknowledgements   vii

Introduction   1

One: The Crack Of Hurling Sticks   3

Two: I Is The Enemy   17

Three: Along Came A Spider . . .   29

Four: Declaration   42

Five: The Bastard Breed   52

Six: The Bounty Was Rich . . .   67

Seven: The Good, The Bad & The Very Ugly   77

Eight: A Year On The Tiles   89

Nine: Sipping Champagne In The Drunk Tank   98

Ten: Cracks In The Armour   106

Eleven: Democracy In Action   120

Twelve: Be Careful What You Wish For   128

Thirteen: Riding Painted Horses   138

Fourteen: A Period Of Adjustment   149

Fifteen: The Dead Arose And Appeared To Many   158

Sixteen: Crawling From The Wreckage   166

Seventeen: You Liver And Learn   172

Eighteen: The Return Of The Mac   179

Nineteen: They Call You Lady Luck . . .   187

Twenty: The Measure Of A Man   193

Discography   199

ACKNOWLEDGEMENTS

For providing additional source material for this book, I would like to offer my enduring gratitude and appreciation to the following individuals: Alan Cross, Andrew Anthony, Andrew Mueller, Andrew Vaughan, Andy Hurt, Annie Nightingale, Anthony Thornton, Antonella Black, Barry Egan, Bill Black, Brian Rohan, Catherine Jackson, Cathi Unsworth, Charles Shaar Murray, Charmaine O'Reilly, Chris Clunn, Colin Irwin, Colm Tóibín, Danny Frost, Danny Kelly, David Cavanagh, David Quantick, David Sinclair, Eddie Doyle, Edwin Pouncey, Elaine McArdle, James Delingpole, Jane Simon, Jim Conlon, Joe Strummer, John Constantine, John Marcus, John Wilde, Johnny Cigarettes, Kathy Burke, Kathy Sweeney, Keith Cameron, Laurence Aston, Marian McKeone, Mark Cooper, Mark Prendergast, Martha Keenes, Michael Dwyer, Michael Sheridan, Mick Brown, Morten Stale Nilsen, Neil Perry, Neil Spencer, Niall Stanage, Nick Moulton, Paul Hill, Peter Paphides, Phil Lawton, Phillip Larkin, Rob Steen, Rose Rouse, Sancha De Burca, Sid Griffin, Simon Mayo, Steph Hendry, Steve Pyke, Stuart Bailie, Stuart Maconie, Tim Peacock, Tom Dunphy, Tonya Henderson & Victoria Clarke. Particular thanks must go to Sean O'Hagan, Gavin Martin & Adrian Deevoy, whose various articles concerning Shane and The Pogues over the years were a source of continued inspiration.

I consulted the following television/radio networks, magazines, newspapers and books during the course of my research, and in some cases extracted interview material. Many thanks then, to *Amplifier*, BBC, *Beat, Daily Mirror, Evening Herald, Loaded, Mojo*, NME, *Q, Rock 'n' Reel*, RTE, *Sunday Business Post, Sunday Tribune, Sunday World, The Correspondent, Daily Telegraph, Guardian, Irish Famine, Irish Post, Irish Voice, Irish World, Observer, Sun, Sunday Independent, Time Out, Uncut & Virgin Encyclopaedia of*

Pop. The same applies to the following magazines which have ceased publication: *Melody Maker* (R.I.P.), *Sounds*, *RCD Magazine* and *Jamming*. I must also express all due appreciation to Ingrid Knetsch and Laurence Clark, who together run *Paddy Rolling Stone – the official Friends of Shane MacGowan web site*. Through their website, I became aware of several Shane related magazine articles of which I had no prior knowledge. As with the above, in some cases I extracted interview material.

Several honourable mentions. First out of the hat is Chris Charlesworth, whose continued patience on this project has surely earned him a place in Heaven. Chris, the drinks and a copy of 'I'm The Face' are on me. As ever, I also remain indebted to Andrew King for providing a sympathetic ear, several articles from *The Twilight Zone* of Eighties publishing and a formidable knowledge of the folk scene. For her overall kindness and continued administrative skills, a king big thanks to Lucy. And last but certainly not least, my gratitude goes to Nikki for always finding the right picture to fit the frame.

On a personal note. To my friends at the top of the road: Jayesh, Viresh and 'Special Brew' Steve. Cheers for the sparkling conversation and beer. To Mrs D (Alice) – you're a good woman. As always, a heartfelt thanks to my wife and parents. And, of course, all thanks to Shane MacGowan himself, for providing 23 years of pure listening pleasure.

INTRODUCTION

For the best part of twenty years, Shane MacGowan has been writing fine songs. Big, fat tuneful songs full of life, death, war and whiskey. Songs that make you proud to be Irish, English or somewhere in between. And most importantly, songs you can return to again and again, safe in the knowledge that while you might have changed, they haven't. In short, he writes songs built to last.

At times, however, it's easy to forget that Shane MacGowan writes songs at all.

Since arriving on the punk scene in 1977 with The Nips, he has become as famous for his lifestyle as his contribution to the art of music. A renowned drinker, Shane's escapades with a bottle are now a matter of public record, his various pub-crawls and binges regularly commented upon in the pages of the national press. As with Charles Bukowski, Jeffrey Bernard, Richard Burton and Oliver Reed, MacGowan's continuing association with drink has often threatened to overwhelm the very talent that brought him to prominence in the first place.

Yet close examination of that talent reveals a body of work perhaps unrivalled in recent folk, or indeed, most pop. By aligning Irish traditional music with his own experiences of fallen souls, wasted lives and the cruelty of the city, MacGowan and his band, The Pogues, resurrected interest in a genre many thought well past commercial resuscitation, dragging it kicking and screaming into the arenas and stadiums of the UK, Eire and the States throughout the Eighties and early Nineties. A joy to behold, The Pogues were a perfect distillation of strong liquor, deceptively good musicianship and punk rock attitude. And Shane was at the very heart of it all – bottle in one hand, microphone in the other. Lauded by critics and fellow performers such as U2, Christy Moore, Bob Dylan and Sinéad O'Connor, MacGowan was seen by many as an able successor to the likes of James Joyce, Flann O'Brien and the immortal Brendan Behan, his undoubted flair for word-play emblematic of Ireland's rich, literary convenant.

"Behan came from the Irish literary tradition of the bard being a drunk, getting paid in whiskey and sleeping in a ditch," Shane once said. "I don't get paid in whiskey and I don't sleep in a ditch, but I see myself metaphorically like that – as coming from that tradition." Of course, like all great romantic images, it wasn't destined to last. Bored by touring and ravaged by drink and drugs, he found himself ousted from The Pogues in 1991. Regarded as a spent force, MacGowan was fully expected to disappear into the musical ether, an entertaining footnote, if nothing else, to the history of Eighties pop. But in typically stubborn fashion, he just kept coming. As did his songs. In truth, they probably will do for some time yet.

The purpose of this book, then, is to examine those songs in accordance with Shane MacGowan's life experience and the culture in which he was raised. After all, according to U2's mercurial frontman, Bono, the two are inextricably linked. "I don't think anyone writes better songs than Shane . . . the words are everything for him. That's where he lives really." From a near idyllic childhood in County Tipperary, Eire to a surprisingly strong solo career in the mid-Nineties, each step of MacGowan's route has been clearly marked in the songs he has written. Street violence and opium dens. Horse races and jail cells. The magic invention of faraway wars to the tramp living on his doorstep, it's all in the songs.

And they're still worth listening to.

ONE

The Crack Of Hurling Sticks

Shane Patrick Lysaght MacGowan was born on Wednesday, December 25, 1957 in Tunbridge Wells, Kent. Some fifty miles away in Buckingham Palace, London, Queen Elizabeth II was making her first Christmas broadcast on television. Understandably, no mention of Shane's arrival was made in her speech. Yet, had she known of his future contribution to the cause of Anglo/Irish relations, the oversight might well have been corrected.

Shane's parents, Maurice and Therese, were actually visiting relatives in England at the time of his birth. Married only a year or so before, the couple met in Dublin, Eire in the early Fifties. Following a recent win in the beauty contest "Colleen of the year", Therese moved to Ireland's capital city from her childhood home of Tipperary to pursue a temporary career in modelling, though she also harboured secret ambitions to become an actress. A native Dubliner, from a middle-class background, Maurice MacGowan was by his own admission 'a local roustabout' when he met his future wife. However, like Therese, he was of an artistic nature and often dreamed of writing a novel. "My mother was a prizewinning folk-singer in her youth," Shane later remembered, "and my father wanted to be an author."

Following their son's birth, the couple returned to Eire to begin a new life. Electing to bring Shane up in the country rather than the city, they moved into Therese's homestead in the parish of Borrisokaine, near Nenagh in north-west Tipperary. Lying in the province of Munster, and bordered by Clare, Limerick and Offaly (amongst others), Tipperary was arguably at the heart of rural Ireland. A small county, its people gleaned their living mainly through agriculture, setting land aside for the grazing of cattle and sheep. Of course there were towns, with Roscrea, Clonmel, Cashel, Carrick-on-Suir and Thurles providing work for non-farm owners. Yet, in the main, Tipperary remained a thoroughly green and largely unspoilt part of Eire.

Beyond its association with 'the land', the county was justly famous for the prowess of its hurling team – an extremely fast field sport played with carved sticks and a tightly wound ball. Since the introduction of national championships in the 1890s, Tipperary had won in excess of twenty 'All-Irelands', placing them behind only Cork and Kilkenny in terms of title victories. Horse racing, too, played a fundamental part in the county's social life, with the track at Limerick Junction visited by thousands of spectators each year. For those drawn to the water, Lough Derg provided fine opportunities for sailing and fishing, with the Lough itself taking its source from Ireland's largest river, the Shannon. In short then, Shane MacGowan was returning to a huge playground, where the most threatening noise to be heard was the crack of hurling sticks and the occasional bark of a collie dog.

Like the county in which he grew up, Shane's childhood home was quintessentially Irish, a pleasing mixture of sturdy, practical furnishings and religious iconography. Overlooking family activity in the living room was a framed picture of the then current Pope, John the XXIII, and a plaster statue of the Sacred Heart of Jesus (an image of Christ with arms outstretched). Beside the dressing table stood a red couch. It was here that MacGowan slept. "There was about 12 people living in the house at one time or another, sleeping three to a bed," he later confirmed. "I used to sleep on the couch, because it was more comfortable. When I was a kid, there was no running water. We had an electric fire and a fire to cook with . . . but no cooker as such. Basic and beautiful. It was the end of an era that I just happened to catch. I'm glad I did."

Shane wasn't exaggerating about the lack of creature comforts in rural Ireland at the beginning of the Sixties. Unlike Eire's capital, Dublin, there was no network of pipes laid to provide running water for the populace. Instead, country dwellings often relied on natural wells and pumps, with water being stored in tanks and barrels outside the house rather than within it. While the MacGowan family were lucky enough to receive electricity from a local grid, many farms in nearby counties such as Clare and Limerick were without even that luxury – the only sources of heat and light provided by firewood and locally grown turf. It was not until the end of the decade that full modernisation of these areas took place.

However, there were always parties to attend. More often than not, they were held by Shane's parents. "There was always music." Therese MacGowan told the BBC. "Every weekend, sometimes even in the middle of the week, we'd have music . . . dancing on the old kitchen floor. And so Shane absorbed all that wonderful traditional culture at a formative age." Often at these family gatherings (or 'sessions'), the young MacGowan was placed upon the kitchen table, and asked to sing. Suffice it to say, he needed little encouragement: "I did my first gig when I was three," he recalled. "I used to like Christmas a lot too, when I was a kid, but as I got older, it lost its appeal. Everyone gradually tended to forget it was my birthday because they were too busy getting drunk together. But so what . . . you can't complain about a piss-up, can you?"

It would appear, then, that Shane MacGowan's earliest childhood memories were entirely bereft of conflict. A small boy growing up in a close-knit community, his days were rich in the enchantment of the time and place, filled with doting relatives, friendly local musicians and curious looking drinks placed just beyond his grasp. Still too young to fully understand the all-pervading influence of the church on Eire's social attitudes and behaviour, let alone the small-mindedness and black cynicism that often accompanied life in the country, Shane's Ireland was an idealised one – "basic, beautiful" and "full of love". "All I ever had were happy times," he later said.

Unfortunately, MacGowan was wrenched from his surroundings at the age of six, another statistic in one of Ireland's most enduring problems: emigration. Since The Great Famine of 1845–49 (when potato crops failed for four years in succession), Eire had seen a steady migration of its young to foreign climes. In the famine years, this exodus was linked entirely to survival, with over a quarter of the country's population (approximately one million people) leaving to seek food and work in the USA and England. To give some indication of the numbers involved, in 1847 alone, over 300,000 Irish citizens arrived in Liverpool, with 116,000 of these described as "half-naked and starving". For those sailing to find a new life, conditions were little short of appalling. Crippled by illnesses such as typhoid and dysentery, the passengers were, in the words of one contemporary government official: "generally crowded or huddled together in the most disgraceful manner imaginable. They were perfectly helpless, covered in filth and dirt and completely drenched by the sea wash." As a consequence, many thousands died on route to their destination, giving birth to the long-held expression "Coffin ship".

Though Ireland's food-chain eventually re-established itself, a precedent for escape had been set in motion. From 1850 to 1870, another one million people would leave the country behind in favour of other English-speaking nations, the US, Canada, Australia and the UK. In truth, there was little to keep them from going. Rocked by continuing economic problems, unemployment, disputes over land and a supreme dissatisfaction with English rule, Eire was a pot all but ready to boil over, its populace either doomed to stay and suffer, or leave while they could. When dissatisfaction erupted into open violence in the fight for Irish independence in 1916, thousands more set sail, this time avoiding bullets rather than the effects of hunger. Even the introduction of the Free State in 1922 and the beginnings of home rule could not stem the tide, with approximately 100,000 more citizens applying for emigrant status in the years between 1930 to 1955.

Thus, when the MacGowans made the decision to move from north-west Tipperary to Brighton, England, they were merely following an established tradition of cultural exodus – seeking, in effect, a prosperity and future that couldn't be found at home. For Shane, who joined his parents later, the experience was jarring. "I didn't want to leave," he said. "No, I *hated* leaving. We lived in Brighton first . . . a terrible place, always cold and windy . . . always grey." To compound the greyness of the skies, MacGowan was also confronted with "complete culture shock. There were black people and big city streets. I'd spent my childhood in a remote part of Ireland. There were lots of hills, small farms and the River Shannon. Lots of traditional musicians. Hurling. Horse racing. I hated it, hated coming to England . . ."

To support his family, Maurice MacGowan had already secured employment with clothing giants C&A, taking on an administrative role in the company's offices. "(My dad) was a pen-pusher, a clerical worker," Shane later confirmed. In due course, his mother also found a job working as a typist in a convent. With his parents now assimilated into the everyday ways of English life, it was time for MacGowan junior to do the same. Nonetheless, Shane's first days in school were not without their difficulties. "Disgust, hatred, fear, loathing . . . (I had) the accent kicked out of me."

Shaken by his surroundings, marked out by his voice and no doubt petrified by what the future held, the six-year-old child could at least turn to his parents and newly born infant sister,

Siobhan, for emotional support. And like most Irish families living in the UK, there was no shortage of aunts, uncles and similarly displaced children to draw solace from. Still, it was only on the frequent trips home that Shane and his younger sibling felt truly free. "In England," Siobhan later recalled, "I was in a constant state of trauma. But when we went back, I let my breath out."

Within a year or so, the MacGowans moved again, this time to Ealing, in West London, where they eventually put down roots. "I never really *settled*," Maurice MacGowan later confirmed. "The English people were great, but the general atmosphere was very puritanical . . . all the right laws, but the wrong application. The Irish are essentially a lawless people, that's what makes us a free people in a way . . ." Obviously experiencing difficulties of his own, Shane's father sought an emotional connection with his homeland via a rapidly expanding collection of LPs, full of traditional Irish Ceilidh (pronounced K-Lee) music. Yet his greatest affection was reserved for The Dubliners, a rambunctious folk group led by Luke Kelly and Ronnie Drew, whose "dirty songs" of "drinking, carousing and the price to be paid the morning after" were stirring up major interest in Ireland at the time.

Drawn to what he heard, Shane was soon sitting alongside his father, humming along to the sounds emanating from the record player. "I was mad on The Dubliners as a kid," he said, "especially the dirty songs." Whether they were a vital link to the fields he left behind or simply an exciting alternative to the joys of TV or tormenting his sister, the eventual result of Shane's infatuation with The Dubliners cannot be understated. As the years came to show, their lyricism and musicianship would inform much of his adult life – from the songs he wrote to the habits he pursued.

However, for the time being at least, MacGowan showed little outward sign of rebellion. Instead, he was thoroughly absorbed with matters of spirit. "(Though) my parents spent the first ten years of my life lapsing and repenting like bloody yo-yos, I stayed a religious maniac until the age of 11." Such devotion to "the Cross" was not uncommon in Irish children. Like Italy, Spain and Poland, Eire's history was symbiotically linked to that of the Church, the nation converting en masse to Catholicism under the guiding hand of St. Patrick in the sixth century. In fact, when Protestantism first swept across Europe in the 1500s, it had little initial impact on Southern Ireland or its people, their faith in Rome too firmly entrenched to be shaken by charges of Papal corruption or abuse of power. As the centuries rolled on, this faith only grew stronger, with thoughts of God and Heaven representing a welcome alternative to the numerous difficulties they faced.

From a formative age then, Irish infants were surrounded by images of Christ, his features dominating weekly church services, the schools they attended and more often than not, the houses in which they grew up. Shane's upbringing was no different, with religious icons taking pride of place in various rooms of his Tipperary home. While his parents may have harboured the occasional doubts regarding the strength of their own religious convictions, the young MacGowan remained ever faithful to "the Holy Spirit". According to him, it was all the fault of his aunt, Nora. "She used to indoctrinate me with loads of Catholic magazines and make me do the Rosary."

The bubble surrounding Shane's innocent notions of Christianity came to an abrupt end while on holiday in Ireland in 1968. "I remember the day I lapsed like it was yesterday, " he later recalled to *Time Out*. "I was walking up a country lane and it just hit me. 'Hang on,' I thought. 'Just supposing it isn't true? Suppose there's no heaven or hell? Suppose there's nothing after death?' I just couldn't get that out of my head . . ." Suffice it to say, any stray thoughts of becoming a priest ended soon after this moment of clarity. However, MacGowan claims that his faith (or a modified version of it), still guides his conscience as an adult. As the saying goes, 'Once a Catholic, always a Catholic . . .'

Beyond his immediate spiritual distress, Shane was discovering another religion of sorts. "My aunt used to smoke, drink and gamble," he later confirmed. "Those were the vices she passed on to me. We used to do the horses, and she'd give me cigarettes and port. Her belief was that if you allow kids to drink what you're drinking in the house, then you don't shroud alcohol in mystique – you stop them becoming alcoholics." Whatever the truth of his aunt's philosophy, the young MacGowan rapidly developed a taste for alcohol, enjoying the combined sense of relaxation and relative abandon it brought. While his parents surely kept all spirits under lock and key, regular visits to his uncle's pub in Dagenham ensured Shane could sneak a quick taste of beer or whiskey when the occasion demanded it. As with so many of his childhood experiences, MacGowan would forge an enduring alliance with alcohol in years to come, its importance to his life perhaps only superseded by a love of music and literature.

It was precisely that love of literature that enabled him to find a way forward in the English educational system. A voracious reader since infancy, Shane quickly dispensed with the likes of *Learn The Alphabet With Janet And John* and *Peter And Jane Go To The Zoo* in favour of his father's book collection. By the age of eight, he was already engrossed in the works of Ian Fleming (the creator of superspy James Bond), and soon after could be found tackling novels by the likes of Joseph Heller and Graham Greene. The Irish poetry of William Butler Yeats and James Donleavy was also diligently poured over. Legend even has it that MacGowan successfully worked his way through James Joyce's magnum opus, *Ulysses.* "Now that took me a while," he later laughed. The discovery of his ultimate literary hero, the hard-drinking Dubliner Brendan Behan only added to Shane's growing interest in the joys of the written word.

Unsurprisingly, this appetite for books soon translated itself into an enviable command of the English language, a fact MacGowan's teachers duly noticed and capitalised on. Sensing a potential prodigy in their midst, Shane was actively encouraged in his essay writing, and (much to his joy) given additional texts to read. Among his accomplishments was a critical analysis of the romantic poet/visionary William Blake that truly propelled him into the literary firmament. He followed this up by composing his own poetry at a tender age. Paying a small bursary to gain entrance to Westminster School, a prestigious fee-paying institution with a superb academic record and teachers to match, 12-year-old Shane MacGowan joined the ranks of the privileged few. He celebrated his good fortune by stealing sufficient money to buy a Jimi Hendrix album.

By this time, Shane's musical tastes had extended well beyond those of his parents with Sixties psychedelic icon Hendrix becoming a firm favourite. "*Axis: Bold As Love* really changed my life," Shane later said of Jimi's 1967 LP. "I nicked it, I think. Or I stole the money to buy it. Records cost two pounds when I was a boy, so I usually bought singles. I got as many as I could for Christmas and birthdays and stuff." Entranced by Hendrix's soulful combination of blues, funk and hard rock stylings, it was only a matter of time before the young MacGowan was connecting the dots to other icons of the era. "Creedence Clearwater Revival, Led Zeppelin, Cream, MC5 right up to The Stooges . . . thousands of 'em. They were raw, real . . . sincere."

Shane's youthful tastes didn't end with straight-ahead rock. There were other, more eclectic avenues to explore including flirtations with Bebop, jump blues and early reggae. However, he saved the lion's share of his praise for two wildly different, yet strangely similar, performers: Bo Diddley and Lou Reed. "Bo Diddley was my favourite black rock'n'roller," MacGowan later told *Melody Maker*. "You never knew what he was going to do . . .

hard rock, lots of guitar solos (or) straight-up blues. What I really liked were the classic records he made in the Fifties and Sixties. Wild stuff. Pure rhythm." Lou Reed invoked a similar response. "A really big influence, but I couldn't pin it down to one record. Anything off the first Velvet Underground album, I suppose." Though he didn't know it at the time, Shane's first band would bear stark witness to his adolescent obsessions with Diddley and Reed, albeit with an extremely punk rock twist in the tail.

Yet back in the early Seventies, he was still amassing new influences. Records by Sam Cooke, Otis Redding, Sly & The Family Stone and Irish group Thin Lizzy were all bought, listened to and duly dissected. "Van Morrison and Lizzy were both really big influences on me. Especially Phil Lynott's writing . . . great songs, great melodies, great lyrics." It was perhaps fitting that MacGowan made a clear emotional connection with Phil Lynott's sinewy, but always romantic, brand of Celtic rock. A black kid raised in a decidedly white (and extremely tough) area of Dublin, Lynott formed Thin Lizzy while still a teenager in 1969, gaining early success with a spirited rendition of the Irish traditional standard 'Whiskey In The Jar'.

By fusing the bump and grind of acts such as Jimi Hendrix and Led Zeppelin to the subtle complexities of Celtic folk, he propelled Thin Lizzy to stardom – the first act since Van Morrison and Rory Gallagher to really escape the confines of Ireland's music scene and ply their trade on an international stage. Additionally, with songs such as 'Vagabond Of The Western World', 'Emerald' and, in later years, 'Black Rose', Lynott cast a sharp eye on the history of Eire, drawing lyrical inspiration from tales of high kings, doomed young warriors, the famine years and political insurrection. As with Lou Reed and Bo Diddley, MacGowan would take inspiration from Phil Lynott's work in times to come, modifying the themes he raised and presenting them in a bold, new fashion.

An inquisitive, gifted teenager, with an ear for good music and a love of "the word", it was perhaps inevitable that Shane MacGowan's next discovery was the recreational use of soft drugs. "As a small boy, I was desperate to learn about things," he confirmed. "I read a lot, not Enid Blyton or any of that shit. I went straight to James Bond and then on to serious litera-ture. The same thing that made me read was what took me to drink and drugs." Already familiar with the joys of alcohol, MacGowan next set his sights on marijuana. Pleased with its effects, it was only a matter of time before he expanded his pharmaceutical horizons to include LSD, or to give it its full name, Lysergic Acid Diethylamide – an artificially created compound renowned for producing hallucinogenic effects when swallowed. Cheap to buy, and relatively fast-acting, LSD fascinated Shane as much as port, beer and whiskey. Unfortu-nately, his teachers at Westminster School took a different view, immediately expelling him when he was arrested for pos-session of drugs in 1971. In later years, MacGowan became convinced that it was his intellect, rather than his fondness for "Acid", that forced Westminster's hand. "I was exceptionally clever," he said. "*That's* the reason why I got kicked out." Perhaps. Perhaps not.

In reality, Shane's expulsion from Westminster was the first public manifestation of a rebel spirit that was destined to recur again and again in the coming years. Still only 14, he had blown a scholarship with one of London's most prestigious schools, marked his card with the educational authorities, and as a result, would be carefully monitored by any institution brave enough to take him on. MacGowan solved the dilemma by tem-porarily turning his back on education altogether, preferring instead to take up a number of menial jobs such as shelf-stacking, warehouseman and, somewhat bizarrely, the position of porter at the Indian Embassy. Lying about his age to secure employment, he drifted from pillar to post for some months before finally succumbing to his parents wishes that he return "to the books". A placing at Hammersmith's College of Further Education soon followed.

However, the once keen English student was now more interested in smoking dope in the common rooms than discussing the merits of Blake and Swift with teachers. Though MacGowan continued to be a voracious reader, literally eating texts by the likes of Steinbeck, Salinger, Hemingway and Runyon, his disgust with the intellectual methodology used to dissect such writers was forcing his attention elsewhere. A firm believer in "feeling a book" rather than subjecting it to endless analysis, Shane had grown profoundly suspicious of his teachers' attempts to distil the essence of literature into a series of largely futile discussions and essays. This penchant for seeking emotional impact from words rather than ascribing them a critical value would inform much of his later work.

Voluntarily releasing himself from Hammersmith, Shane returned to the workplace, this time settling into the role of apprentice barman in an Irish pub. However, his tenure as "a bottle-washer and cellar-man" proved all too brief: "I got the sack for turning up late and being pissed on the job." His options now running perilously low, MacGowan made further overtures towards the catering industry, or more specifically, the mobile catering industry. "I got a job as a meals-on-wheels delivery man in Maida Vale," he later confirmed. "You'd walk in and find a stiff that had been lying in its own piss and shit for weeks." Suffice it to say, he left soon after.

Though Shane was finding it hard to hold down a job, his days remained largely entertaining – either spent in the pub, or alternatively, experimenting with drugs in the homes of a few close friends. Allegations persist that during this time he fell in with a bunch of "posh kids from Hampstead", who "smoked pot and talked utter shit." Other sources have MacGowan firmly placed in Islington, Holloway Road and most frequently Kings Cross, drinking with anyone and everyone who crossed his path.

Whatever the truth, his experiments with both drugs and alcohol had reached a crescendo by late 1974, leading to the 17-year-old MacGowan's admission to St. Mary of Bethlehem Hospital in Central London.

Renowned in the 19th century for its treatment of the mentally ill (the hospital was originally nicknamed "Bedlam", a word now commonly used to describe scenes of uproar or great disturbance) St. Mary of Bethlehem circa 1975 specialised in the rehabilitation of alcoholics and drug users, offering medication and therapy to those in danger of dying from their addictions. Though it remains debatable whether Shane fell into this category, he nevertheless spent six months at St. Mary's, with doctors "trying to get me off the acid, the booze, the dope and the pills." It was a trying time for both MacGowan and his family. He was eventually released with a clean bill of health, though he fell off the wagon again almost immediately. Sadly, it was a process he was doomed to repeat over and over again in his adult life.

Back on the streets again, Shane found himself increasingly drawn to London's live music circuit. In fact, his first in-concert experience had occurred as early as 1971, witnessing glam-rockers Mott The Hoople perform at the Fulham Greyhound. Yet it was a flourishing R&B scene that caught his attention this time. Excited by the earthy groove of acts such as Dr. Feelgood and Eddie & The Hot Rods, MacGowan felt at home amongst the beer and the decibels – the pungent intimacy offered by venues like Islington's Hope And Anchor a far cry from the white walls and crisp sheets of St. Mary's. Obviously addicted to this new rush, he became a regular (and exceedingly) enthusiastic face in the crowd, tracking bands he liked and walking out on those he didn't. Nonetheless, concert tickets didn't come cheap. Employment had therefore to be procured to fund his new-found habit. It came soon enough, with a semi-regular position as sales assistant at Rocks Off Records, a stall buried deep in

Soho's Berwick Street market. Here, MacGowan was free to indulge his love of listening to albums, tapes and the occasional bootleg and, more importantly, get paid for it. Life, as they say, was good.

It was about to get markedly better.

TWO

I Is The Enemy

On April 3, 1976, Shane MacGowan attended a gig at Central London's Nashville Rooms. The headline act was a fast-paced little outfit called The 101ers, led by John Mellor and Clive Temperley. Formed some two years before, the band were fairly typical exponents of 'pub rock' – a twitchy amalgam of Fifties R&B, hot-wired guitars and thumping percussion values. As MacGowan was already a fan of the similarly themed Dr. Feelgood, he must have had a fair idea of what to expect from the evening ahead. Instead, he experienced an epiphany. "I'd gone to see The 101ers at the Nashville," he later recalled, "and The Sex Pistols were the support band. I just couldn't believe it. *This* was the band I'd been waiting for. I thought, 'This is what I'm all about.' So I started following them." In the space of some 30 minutes, Shane MacGowan became a punk. And as time would show, he was really rather good at it.

Given MacGowan's overwhelming reaction to The Sex Pistols and the effect they had on his life, it is worth investigating the early history of the group and their manager/arch nemesis Malcolm McLaren. Suffice it to say, clothing shop owner and part-time svengali McLaren learnt much while in the USA in 1975. As latter-day manager of ailing scuzz-rockers The New York Dolls, he was introduced to a sound and scene of astonishing vitality with Patti Smith, The Ramones, The

17

Dead Boys and Television all making their live débuts in clubs such as Manhattan's justly infamous CBGBs. Unlike the bloated supergroups of the day, these acts rejected all pretension in favour of a stripped down, high-octane three-chord formula. Songs went by in seconds rather than hours, and featured little in the way of instrumental embellishment. No endless guitar or drum solos, no Bach-like keyboard runs, and absolutely no mention of *The Hobbit* or *Lord Of The Rings*. In short, just meat, bones and a lot of attitude. Thrilling stuff indeed.

When MacLaren eventually returned home to his London fashion store, Sex (at 430 The King's Road, Fulham), he was keen to bring a sense of New York with him. Taking partial inspiration from the "distressed" clothing worn by Television bassist Richard Hell, Malcolm (in conjunction with designer Vivienne Westwood) introduced a line of torn, abused T-shirts and bondage trousers, often replete with obscene slogans and illustrations. The idea was to shock and it worked, drawing a new breed of fairly anarchic teenagers to his shop. One such visitor was a London-Irish youth, John Lydon who, in the course of one balmy August afternoon, not only met McLaren but also two local musicians named Steve Jones and Paul Cook. Learning that Malcolm was attempting to put a group together for guitarist Jones and drummer Cook, Lydon promptly auditioned as vocalist, singing along to a jukebox rendition of either Alice Cooper's 'School's Out' or 'I'm Eighteen', though not even The Sex Pistols themselves seem quite sure. Impressed by his talent, and overuse of TV comedian Dick Emery's catch-phrase, "You're rotten you are . . . but I like you," Jones nick-named Lydon "Johnny Rotten" and McLaren offered him the job of singer. The band's line-up was completed by Malcolm's occasional assistant, bassist Glen Matlock. In tribute to his shop, McLaren christened his new protégés The Sex Pistols.

With The New York Dolls consigned to rock'n'roll heaven,

McLaren was fully able to concentrate his efforts on grooming The Sex Pistols for stardom. Again consulting his 'Manhattan punk' rule book, he encouraged the band to wear clothes from his store, cut their hair in spikes rather than layers and be as obnoxious as humanly possible. As they would soon illustrate to the world, The Sex Pistols needed little encouragement in this area, cultivating an attitude accurately described by one critic as "25% bored, 25% dismissive, and 50% fucking hostile". Behind the scenes, Rotten, Jones and the others worked hard at capturing a sound, taking musical inspiration from the likes of Iggy Pop & The Stooges, early Who and Phil Spector's "wall of sound". With Matlock providing the lion's share of songs (and surprisingly melodic they were too), the quartet were ready for live performance by the end of 1975. Making their début at St. Martin's Art School on November 6, The Sex Pistols lasted an august 10 minutes before the plug was pulled by nervous officials. It was enough. The era of 'No Future' had begun.

By the time Shane MacGowan witnessed the group in April, 1976, The Pistols were only months away from becoming 'Public Enemy No. 1', their combination of raw, under-rehearsed garage-rock and seething lyrical bile soon to bring them into opposition with record companies, TV stations and, eventually, heads of state. To Shane's enduring credit, he understood what they represented within seconds – a blunt-edged sword taking bloody swipes at everything from the monarchy and government to teenage abortion and Nazi concentration camps. "They were the best rock'n'roll band of all time," he later confirmed. "You know . . . just brilliant. And Rotten's lyrics were the cherry on the cake. A lot of the time, he was just taking the piss, which is fair enough (because) the music industry deserves to have the piss taken out of it. But they really did sum up what being a teenager was like in the late Seventies."

That they did. In fact, The Sex Pistols acted as a perfect mirror for adolescent dissatisfaction in England's green and increasingly unpleasant land. As inflation, unemployment and bankruptcy figures rocketed to new levels under the awkward leadership of a marginalised Labour government, the average British youth faced, at best, an uncertain future. To give an example, only two days after The Sex Pistols forever modified Shane MacGowan's brain chemistry at the Nashville Rooms, exhausted Prime Minister Harold Wilson stood down in favour of James Callaghan, a renowned moderate drafted into power in an attempt to curb his party's potentially vote-destroying move to "the extremities of socialism". Elsewhere, Liberal leader Jeremy Thorpe was facing "a sustained press witch hunt and campaign of utter denigration" over allegations that he once indulged in a homosexual affair with former male model Norman Scott. By May 10, 1976, Thorpe was gone, replaced by the more media friendly Scotsman David Steel, the son of a Presbyterian minister.

With such well-respected politicians as John Stonehouse serving time for fraud and deception, 68 arrests and over 500 people injured at Notting Hill's annual carnival and British soldiers accused of "unjust treatment and torture" on the streets of Belfast by the European Court of Human Rights, 19th century poet William Blake's dream of a "new Albion" seemed lost in a mire of bungled statesmanship, inter-racial violence and the re-ignition of centuries old feuds. Only Queen Elizabeth II, soon approaching her Silver Jubilee, proved immune from prosecution. And thanks to the efforts of Malcolm McLaren's unholy little quartet, even that wasn't going to last for long. Faced with such tomfoolery and the prospect of worse to come, it was only fitting that UK youth decided to throw in their lot with The Sex Pistols and begin the process of fighting back.

As a movement, punk grew at a frightening rate with bands forming on an almost daily basis. In May, 1976, Chris Miller (Rat Scabies), Ray Burns (Captain Sensible) and Brian Robertson (Brian Jones) recruited Hemel Hempstead gravedigger

Dave Letts (Dave Vanian) into their ranks to become The Damned, making their first live appearance as support act to The Sex Pistols at Oxford Street's 100 club on July 6. Over in West London, 101ers singer John Mellor finally gave up the ghost of R&B and accepted an invitation to front The Clash, an outfit destined to make almost as much of an impact on the music scene as The Sex Pistols themselves. In keeping with punk's trend of ditching given names in favour of something a little more memorable, Mellor christened himself Joe Strummer – a partial tribute to his manic rhythm guitar style. Not to be outdone, Shane MacGowan took on board the actions of his new heroes and became Shane O'Hooligan. "People used to have aliases back then," he later recalled. "Johnny Rotten, Joe Strummer, Sid Vicious, Billy Idol. You knew they weren't real names, but everyone had to have them."

Despite the fact that Shane wasn't even in a band, he threw himself into punk with an enthusiasm that beggared belief, rapidly becoming one of *the* faces on the London scene. Decked out in a garish Union Jack suit, bright red shirt, brothel creepers and extra skinny tie, O'Hooligan attended almost every gig he could afford to get into, and some he couldn't. As the groups continued to multiply, so did Shane's busy social schedule. He was an almost permanent fixture at The Roxy and 100 Club, where on September 20, he witnessed the live début of Subway Sect and Siouxsie & The Banshees (featuring future Sex Pistol Sid Vicious on drums). Yet, it was an incident at London's ICA Theatre on October 23, 1976 that managed to drag Shane O'Hooligan off the dance floor and into the pages of the music press.

While watching The Clash perform one of their insanely energetic live sets, a suitably animated Shane became involved in a good-natured scuffle with a fellow female audience member. However, things took a turn for the worse when the girl cut his ear open with "some sort of device". As the blood ran, so the cameras flashed and O'Hooligan found himself a featured article in the following week's music papers, fronting accusations of "cannibalistic behaviour" at punk gigs. The truth of the matter was far more innocuous. Shane's ear was cut, but not as reported, severed from his head. "There was a scratching and eventually cutting going on, but that was like a punk thing so it was fairly normal," he later confirmed. "There just happened to be a photographer there when it happened, so they got a picture with my ear bleeding and said it had been bitten off. There was quite a lot of blood but in the end it was all friendly." His assailant, Jane, from future all-girl group The Modettes, unsurprisingly escaped prosecution. Nonetheless, Shane was now a made man and within weeks of the incident, photographed for the front cover of *Sounds*, his wild-eyed stare emblematic of the threat punk posed to Britain's youth. Suffice it to say, he loved the attention. "I was incredibly happy during punk," he once said. "Some called it chaos. I didn't. I called it natural living."

Inevitably, the movement couldn't stay hidden in London's clubs for much longer. Yet, when punk did break into the national consciousness, it did so in quite spectacular fashion. On December 1, 1976, The Sex Pistols appeared as guests on ITV's early evening current affairs programme *Tonight*. Sitting opposite their host, Bill Grundy, the group and their entourage (including Siouxsie Sioux) fielded an increasingly inane series of questions regarding punk's image, politics and philosophy before lapsing into bored stares and giggles. Obviously irritated by their appearance and behaviour, Grundy began goading his charges, with the result that The Pistols let fly with a string of casual obscenities. Incredulous but seemingly amused, Grundy hastily concluded the interview.

By the morning of December 2, The Sex Pistols were "the most hated men in Britain", their grinning faces staring out from news-stands up and down the country. Ecstatic over the media coup (and no doubt ready to start counting coins),

Malcolm McLaren threw fat into the flames when responding to Bill Grundy's accusation that he managed "a foul-mouthed set of yobs". "Of course they're yobs," said a grinning McLaren, "and proud of it." While Grundy eventually lost his job over the incident, The Sex Pistols went from strength to strength, using their new-found notoriety to negotiate contracts with both EMI and A&M Records. Predictably however, both companies grew tired of the group's antics, and dropped them – but not without losing over £125,000 in already paid advances to McLaren. An eventual home was found for The Sex Pistols at Richard Branson's Virgin Records.

That The Sex Pistols benefited immeasurably from their appearance on *Tonight* was beyond doubt. Yet the fall-out of their shock tactics on fans of punk was another thing altogether. Now associated with "those foul-mouthed yobs", supporters of the movement were easily identified by their choice of haircut, penchant for safety pins, and worse still, the clubs they attended. Those with a grievance against punk in general, Johnny Rotten in particular, or indeed, anyone who looked like him could therefore find and eliminate their prey without any great effort. Predictably, dozens of punks, including Shane O'Hooligan received a beating or two for their troubles. "Quite a violent year, 1976," Shane later recalled. "Fingers-up type music, fingers-up type attitude. There was a vacant, nihilistic feeling (all around). I connected with it." Indeed, The Sex Pistols themselves became victims of such violence, with Rotten and Cook attacked by gangs wielding razors and iron bars in the summer of 1977.

One distinctly negative aspect of punk was the hard drugs that fuelled both the bands and their supporters, with substance abuse reaching almost epidemic proportions. "My generation were on hard drugs," said Shane. "A fucking epidemic of hard drug abuse . . . mainly downers, barbiturates and Mandrax." When heroin, amphetamines, solvents and cheap acid were added to a list that already included casual beatings,

violent clashes with police and the continuing threat of retri-
bution from detractors of the movement, being a punk wasn't
the easiest of career choices to make. Of course, Shane persevered. Hopelessly infatuated with The Sex Pistols and what
they represented, he continued to position himself at the forefront of things, trawling London's pubs and clubs in an effort
to find another great band for another great night. It is precisely this Shane who briefly appears in Don Lett's film, *Punk
Rock Movie*, wind-milling madly in front of The Jam as they performed at Victoria's Venue club in the spring of 1977.

By the time The Sex Pistols actually released their début
album, *Never Mind The Bollocks, Here's The Sex Pistols* in November, 1977, the UK was absolutely awash with punk groups.
From X-Ray Spex, The Buzzcocks and The Adverts to Sham
69, Penetration and Chelsea, any musician brave enough to
learn three chords (or in some cases, considerably less) was
taking to the stage only to find themselves covered in spittle
within the space of a minute. Taking their cue from Johnny
Rotten, these acts sang about loss of identity, of serial killers
and the right to work. But the main subject at hand was termi-
nal boredom. In many ways, such protests were artificial – the
battle cries of teenagers too inexperienced in the ways of life
to know what true boredom was. Yet, for the most part, punk
remained a hugely enjoyable and exceedingly energetic alternative to the tales of mid-life crises groups like Pink Floyd were
committing to vinyl.

Behind the scenes, however, punk's true essence was dying.
In reality, the movement was doomed to failure when major
labels sent their A&R men into the clubs and pubs with
cheque books in hand. The Sex Pistols, who at one time promised so much to so many, were now on the verge of collapse,
the group's once bright future blighted by internal squabbles,
drug addiction and Johnny Rotten's growing hatred of
Malcolm McLaren's management style. By January 14, 1978, it
was all over bar the shouting. After completing a set at San

Francisco's Winterland Ballroom, Rotten asked the audience, "Ever get the feeling you've been cheated?" before leaving the stage and the band for good. Though The Pistols continued in one form or another for three months, they were little more than a headless chicken, still unaware its head had been cut from its body.

Nonetheless, the movement started by McLaren and Rotten continued to provide real dividends for those sailing along in their wake. The Clash, The Jam and The Stranglers were all battling their way into the charts and with a second wave of acts already poised on the horizon, punk (or new wave as it was soon to be called) showed little sign of commercial abatement. Shane O'Hooligan certainly thought so, as he was already prowling the stages of Central London as frontman with The Nipple Erectors. A charmingly titled and notoriously unstable outfit who came together in a series of fits and starts during the spring of 1977, The Nipple Erectors comprised Shane on vocals and Shanne Bradley on bass, alongside various ever-changing guitarists and drummers. Playing their first gig at the Roxy in July, 1977, the group were fairly typical exponents of "bog-standard shouty punk", but soon showed signs of improvement, pursuing a melodic quality few acts at that time were brave enough to attempt.

By the time The Sex Pistols finally fell on their sword in April, 1978, The Nipple Erectors were gearing up to release their first single 'King Of The Bop' on Soho Records. Arriving in shops in a garish day-glo cover, with a picture of an open-mouthed, black-clad Shane in the right-hand corner of the sleeve, 'King Of The Bop' was a fair attempt on the group's part to capture both the spirit of punk and rockabilly, the song coming across as a weird composite of The Velvet Underground, The Clash and Sun Records-period Elvis Presley. Though 'King . . .' failed to catapult the band into the Top Thirty, it did act as an able advertisement for their shows, which included opening for punk legend Johnny Moped at Camden Town's Music Machine on May 25, 1978. However, as eager as they were to play live, The Nipple Erectors were constantly being turned away by promoters due to their sexually charged name. "We soon realised we didn't stand a chance in hell of getting anywhere with a name like that," Shane later recalled.

Unlike The Varicose Veins, The Snivelling Shits, Schoolgirl Bitch and The Nosebleeds, The Nipple Erectors decided to modify their epithet to the far more user-friendly The Nips. As the name changed so did the line-up, with Larry Hinrichs and Arcane departing to be replaced by Fritz and Gerry Mackleduff on guitar and drums respectively. This version of the group cut two further singles, the moderately pleasing 'All The Time In The World', and the quite splendid 'Gabrielle'. Written by Shane, 'Gabrielle' jarred uneasily with the spirit of punk, its bold use of harmony proving once and for all he wasn't just listening to The Sex Pistols for purposes of inspiration. "Let's go down the old West End," sang a restrained sounding Shane, "where we used to go when you were my best friend, take a No. 73 to the City."

The old ways were firmly back in place, however, with the release of The Nips' début LP, *Only Happy At The Beginning,* in October, 1980. Featuring the likes of 'Fuss 'N' Bother', 'Stupid Cow' and the aptly titled 'Venus In Bovver Boots', *Only Happy . . .* was a snot-nosed little record, its contents ably captured by Shane's informative sleeve-notes. "The Nips," he wrote, "are about healthy teenage subjects such as sex, violence and getting pissed." All meritable in their own way perhaps, but when one compared The Nips' juvenile sensibilities to the high-mindedness of emergent acts such as Magazine, XTC and Simple Minds, the band appeared old-fashioned and somewhat coarse. Unfortunately, in the time it took Shane to assemble a group, stabilise its line-up, write an album's worth of songs and commit them to posterity, punk's appeal had largely withered, leaving him sounding as redundant as his recently acquired surname.

The sad part of the equation was that Shane knew it. Though he was wholly committed to the punk ethos, he was also aware times were changing – a fact brought home with crushing force at a Joy Division gig in 1979. "I remember watching Joy Division, and it was fucking terrifying, you know?" he later confirmed. "It was like a horror film . . . you were scared to go for a piss in case you missed something. Ian Curtis was clearly disturbed, but still managed to exorcise his demons on-stage." A patron saint of the new wave, Curtis' protests were far more subtle, yet no less affecting than those offered by Johnny Rotten. Both disenchanted romantic and terrified witness, Joy Division's troubled frontman was an arbiter of things to come, his lyrical themes of rigorous self-examination and crushed love a startling alternative to punk tales of unemployment, boredom and imminent civil war. Sadly, Curtis hung himself in May, 1980.

In the face of such corrosive change, it was perhaps fitting that The Nips decided to break up around the time of the release of *Only Happy At The Beginning*. Though the group struggled hard through numerous line-up changes (they even employed future Pogue James Fearnley on rhythm guitar for a time) and limited support from the music press, their fate had been more or less decided when The Sex Pistols imploded on stage some three years before. No matter how quaint the notion "Punk meets Ted" sounded on paper, the birth of new wave and synthetic pop left them largely without purpose. Years later, Shane would sum up his time with The Nips in a single sentence. "We were all right, I suppose, but nothing to write home about . . ." Yet, MacGowan had learned much from his time with the band. Taking on board punk's 'Do it yourself' message, he temporarily escaped into a new world of possibility, confirming his talents as a singer and songwriter and proving, once and for all, there was a life beyond stacking shelves. More importantly, it had been fun.

Placing Shane O'Hooligan aside for the moment, MacGowan temporarily returned to his duties as an assistant at Rocks Off

Records, now a shop located in Central London's Hanway Street rather than a stall in the heart of Soho. Here he was free to dwell on the past, plan for the future and crucially, listen to as many records as he liked. "I was happy enough," he said. "Every now and again, the shop would fill up with people and I'd be rushed off my feet, but you couldn't really whinge about it. I was getting paid to listen to records. That was better than working on a building site or being a mini-cab driver." Obviously, the notion of being "a mad bastard singing punky ceilidh music" hadn't quite occurred to him yet . . .

THREE

Along Came A Spider . . .

"The only reason we started playing this kind of music is because no other fucker was doing it."

– Shane MacGowan

Like many successful bands, The Pogues emerged from a swamp of old friendships, loose connections and sheer bloody coincidence. There was no magic formula to follow, just a rough idea that eventually took shape in the pubs and clubs of Central London. Suffice it to say, Shane MacGowan was at the heart of it, but not wholly responsible for weaving the tale. That process took teamwork, the kindness of strangers and a whole lot of drink.

Since the halcyon days of punk, Shane had been friendly with another ambitious, if misdirected youth by the name of Peter 'Spider' Stacy. Born on December 14, 1958, Stacy was actually a native of Eastbourne, Sussex, but found himself drawn to the capital when bands such as The Sex Pistols and The Clash started gigging at the 100 Club, the ICA and the now legendary Roxy. He first crossed paths with MacGowan in 1977 at Camden Town's cavernous Roundhouse venue. "It was at a Ramones gig," Spider later recalled, "and Shane was crawling around out of his brains on the steps outside. He said to me, 'Y'aving a good time, are ya?' I went, 'Yeah,' so he said,

'That's what it's all about innit?' He sort of stood by that philosophy . . ."

A friendship duly formed, the pair soon found themselves fronting separate bands. While MacGowan experimented with his fusion of "Rockabilly meets punk" in The Nips, Stacy was content to create "sheer bloody havoc" as part of The Millwall Chainsaws, a "punk meets punk" outfit principally famous for racing through their set at mach speed before completely thrashing their equipment and heading for the bar. When the mood took him, Shane would join the Chainsaws on-stage, providing backing vocals and occasional guitar. More often than not though, his contribution amounted to avoiding flying drumsticks (courtesy of Chainsaws percussionist Ollie) or tripping over various leads, bottles and microphone stands. "The Chainsaws," said one witness to these events, "were brilliant, but shit."

By 1981, both MacGowan and Stacy were off the live music circuit altogether, with Shane happily ensconced at Rocks Off Records and Spider allegedly selling used cars to make ends meet. Nonetheless, they remained close friends and could often be found irritating the patrons of various Kings Cross and Holloway Road pubs. "We'd both played in punk bands," MacGowan recalled, "but when we went drinking together, we'd always be thrown out of pubs for singing Irish songs. After a while, we decided to do it on stage so we could get paid for it." As with many epiphanies, neither Shane nor Spider could recall the exact moment when the idea first came to them. However, Stacy never forgot the initial sensation. "The idea of playing punky Ceilidh music came to us like Archimedes in the bath. A few people had touched on the notion before, but nobody had seen it through. Combining the two seemed so . . . blindingly obvious."

In reality, the notion of melding Irish traditional folk and punk rock was neither "blindingly obvious" nor particularly easy to achieve. At its best, Ceilidh music was an art form all its own. Centuries in the making, it was usually performed by highly accomplished players on acoustic instruments such as violins, flutes, uillean pipes and accordions. Lightning fast (as with jigs), more moderately paced (as with reels) or slow and seductive (as with airs), the genre took its roots from 19th century composers such as Carolan and Cearbhail O'Dalaigh. It was modified in the mid-20th century via the endeavours of Sean O'Riada, The Coleman Brothers, Silver Star, The Bothy and Tulla Ceilidh Bands and finally presented in seamless form by The Chieftains, Joe Burke and De Dannen in the Seventies and beyond.

Yet, like any music "born of court and feast", Ceilidh was as much owned by the people as it was the privileged few. In fact, many of the most enduring compositions associated with Irish traditional folk were written not for the banquet or dining hall but for the dance floor or 'feis'. Placed in the hands of peasant musicians, jigs and reels became more lively, while slow, sorrowful airs mirrored the suffering of the land and its populace. When lyrics were eventually added to these melodies, they more often than not portrayed Irish dissatisfaction with English rule, giving birth to the "rebel song" – a form of none too subtle protest directed at continuing British interests in Irish affairs. With this addition firmly in place, Ceilidh could now be enjoyed as both a stately art form, presenting the subtleties and nuances of the tune itself, or as a simple, yet devastatingly effective, record of cultural change. In this respect, Ceilidh was Ireland's version of the blues – a music steeped in history and pageant, protest and revolt.

It was precisely this aspect of Ceilidh with which old punks like MacGowan and Stacy could identify. While the duo could never hope to emulate the technical prowess of groups like The Chieftains or The Bothy Band, they could approximate the simpler pleasures of The Dubliners and The Clancy Brothers, whose homages to the pint pot and the barmaid were bashed out on acoustic guitars, penny whistles and inexpensive fiddles.

Shane was already well familiar with Irish folk's rich back catalogue, having been brought up on a staple diet of traditional
airs and breathless reels. Yet, Spider was a native Englishman,
whose only real exposure to the music of Ireland came via his
friend's album collection. "My introduction to Irish music," he
later said, "really came from sitting in Shane's room, getting
drunk and listening to his dad's Dubliners records." Evidently,
these sessions proved fruitful, as Stacy soon purchased a penny
whistle of his own, fighting daily battles with six holes, five
fingers and a mouthpiece to ensure even the most perfunctory
command of the "tortuous little instrument".

By October, 1982, the pair felt sufficiently confident to foist
their drunken rehearsals on the paying public. However,
instead of approaching an Irish landlord sympathetic enough
to let them play in the back room of his pub, MacGowan and
Stacy chose to make their live début in a 'New Romantic'
nightclub. "It was the era of one faggot and a guy on a
synthesiser," Shane told *Sounds*' Bill Black. "And we used to go
down Cabaret Futura . . . a cheap poseurs place Richard
Strange used to run. Basically, we'd terrorise people into
buying us drink and take the piss out of anyone who was there.
Anyway, we thought we were better than the usual dross, so we
sent our mate Ollie up to Richard to ask if we could do a set of
Irish tunes. Being a diamond geezer, he loved the idea, so we
played a set." Unfortunately for MacGowan, Stacy and Ollie,
their choice of material clashed rather badly with the audience at hand. "The place was packed with squaddies on leave
from the army," Spider later recalled, "and there we were,
singing (Irish rebel songs) like 'The Bold Fenian Men', 'The
Patriot's Game', the whole fucking canon! They started
pelting us with chips and eventually we got the plug pulled on
us. We went down well with the raincoat brigade though . . ."
"Yeah," Shane deadpanned. "They *gave* us chips . . ."

Another witness suitably transfixed with their efforts that
night was Jeremy Max Finer. Born on July 20, 1954 in Stoke-

on-Trent, Staffordshire, Finer was an Oxford University Computer Studies graduate who came to London in the late Seventies, only to find himself sharing a Euston squat with MacGowan and Stacy. "I knew Shane for about six months before I knew he had anything to do with music," he later confirmed. "One night he said he was going off to a gig, but I thought he was going to watch until somebody told me he sang with The Nips." At the beginning of their friendship, MacGowan was mightily impressed with Finer's encyclopaedic knowledge of old country and bluegrass records. "I was completely besotted with country," Finer told *NME*'s Sean O'Hagan. "The stuff I really liked was from the Fifties and Sixties, Jimmy Rogers through to Hank Williams . . . all that romanticism, bums, broken hearts and booze." To reduce the gap between himself and his heroes, Jem took up banjo – a hobby that soon became serious enough for Shane to invite him on the occasional busking trip to Finsbury Park Station. Following the events of Cabaret Futura, it was only a matter of time before MacGowan extended the invitation to include his latest project. Seizing the opportunity with both hands, a pick and four strings, Finer gratefully accepted the offer.

Now calling themselves The New Republicans (a none too subtle reference to late 19th/early 20th century Irish freedom fighters), MacGowan, Stacy and Finer began the process of picking up the occasional gig "here and there". Aside from their semi-regular busking sessions at London tube stations, the trio also appeared in various "Irish-friendly" pubs across the capital, as well as extending their horizons to Wakefield and Leeds, where they performed at The Pindar. As the months went by, so the line-up expanded. First on board was former Nips rhythm guitarist James Fearnley. Born in Manchester on October 10, 1954, the twenty-eight-year-old Fearnley was brought up in Yorkshire but, like his colleagues, was soon lured to London by the promise of 'punk'. It hadn't all gone according to plan though, as he was the first to admit. "I got a job portering in St. Bart's hospital," James later confirmed, "and I moved up the scale to morgue attendant. There was babies popping out of women, guys dying with their heads through windscreens . . . it was horrific."

Sensing his destiny didn't lie in medicine, Fearnley became a semi-permanent fixture on the Kings Cross pub scene, making his way through various groups in search of a break. Having served time with a late incarnation of The Nips, MacGowan was fully aware of James' skills with the guitar, but more interested in his proficiency as an accordionist, a discipline that could be used to full effect with The New Republicans. At first, Fearnley was decidedly ambiguous about throwing in his lot with Shane's latest band. In fact, he was preparing to write a novel at the time of MacGowan's call-up. Yet, when it became clear the group's infrequent concert schedule wouldn't clash too heavily with his literary ambitions, Fearnley climbed on board. Suffice it to say, the book remains unwritten.

Following hot on the heels of Fearnley came another veteran of the Kings Cross scene, drummer Andrew Ranken. A native Londoner, born on November 13, 1953, Ranken was allegedly something of a hippie before joining the group, dividing his time between singing in various pick-up outfits and dabbling in fine art. Nonetheless, legend has it that he was persuaded to "take to the drum stool" (following original percussionist Ollie's departure) after Shane bought him a pint of Carlsberg lager. However unlikely the story is (and it is unlikely), Ranken soon earned the nickname 'The Clobberer' from his fellow bandmates – a suitable appraisal of his minimalist, yet ferocious style. "Andrew's like some kind of glistening steel worker," said an obviously admiring Fearnley, "bashing seven shades of shit out of his drums . . ."

With all this testosterone swimming around, it was perhaps inevitable that the final musician to join The New Republicans should be a woman. And so it was that Caitlin 'Rocky' O'Riordan completed the six-piece line-up in the winter of

1982. Previously bassist with indie hopefuls The Pride Of The Cross, the wild-haired O'Riordan shared MacGowan's decidedly Irish roots and, equally as important, his ability to drink "with the best of them". Playing with a tight, economical style, she claimed Elvis Costello as her primary musical influence on arrival in the group, though also admitted "he's a bit fat at the moment, like Robert DeNiro in *Raging Bull*". This blunt assessment of Costello's girth would come back to haunt her in quite splendid fashion within the space of just three years.

Though The New Republicans owned records by Tom Waits, The Stooges, The Velvet Underground, Elvis Costello and rather bizarrely, Big Country, they stayed more or less faithful to MacGowan's and Stacy's original remit of playing "punky Ceilidh". But even here, the influences were steadily growing. "We'd (listen to) Christy Moore, Planxty, The Dubliners, The Clancy Brothers, The Chieftains," Shane later recalled. "There were millions of them, right through to Brendan Shine and Big Tom." Ably dissecting the best and worst Irish music had to offer, the group's in-concert playlist duly expanded to include the likes of 'Greenland Whale Fisheries', 'Whiskey, You're The Devil' and that joyous ode to the pleasures of working on a building site, 'Muirshin Durkin'. To ensure variety, they even threw in a cover of Kris Kristofferson's hoary old country standard, 'Me And Bobby McGhee'.

By January, 1983, three major changes had taken place within the group. While it was generally agreed Spider Stacy would act as The New Republicans' lead vocalist, his on-stage behaviour meant that Shane was being increasingly relied upon to sing. "Spider was always meant to be our frontman," MacGowan remembered, "but he kept falling over and I used to stay standing up, so I ended up the one who got the attention." In addition to his strong centre of gravity, Shane was also starting to write songs for the band. "It's a bit like Lou Reed," he said by way of explanation. "All his songs are like little bits of New York. Well, that's all mine are really, songs about people you meet in the pub . . ." Natural modesty aside, MacGowan's abilities as a songwriter and surprisingly adept vocalist placed him at the epicentre of the group, allowing him to exert a clear influence over musical direction and live performance – a fact, coincidentally, critics were not slow to pick up upon.

"They suffer from disorganisation, scrappiness and long periods of tuning up between songs," wrote *NME*'s Gavin Martin of one of the band's earliest performances. "Yet, Shane has a fine singing voice, (being) one of the few people this side of forty who can actually use their voice expressively and draw you into places and feelings sketched out in the songs. But are they taking themselves seriously enough to make a real go of it? After all, 'Pogue Mahone' is Gaelic for 'Kiss My Hole'."

The last real change The New Republicans made was to ditch their politically contentious name in favour of the delightfully Irish 'Pogue Mahone'. As Gavin Martin suggested in his review, the phrase literally meant 'Kiss My Arse' in Ireland's native language, and had long been the insult of choice in bars and pubs across the land. Of course, in England 'Pogue Mahone' meant precious little to anyone, with concert promoters remaining largely unaware of its dubious connotations. This fact was driven home in amusing fashion when venues such as Islington's Hope And Anchor and The Fulham Greyhound proudly advertised upcoming appearances by the band in the music press, often misspelling the name completely. Depending on the week, Pogue Mahone became 'Poguemahones', 'Poglle Mahone' or, worse still, 'Pogle Mogle'.

Temporarily escaping the attention of censors, the newly christened Pogue Mahone continued to build up a live following around London, establishing weekend residencies at the Hope And Anchor, Kentish Town's Bull And Gate and Harlesden's Mean Fiddler throughout 1983. The group also plied their wares at Camden Dingwalls and Oxford Street's 100 Club as well as small pubs and clubs up and down the M1.

However, a breakthrough of sorts occurred when they appeared at the Camden Town's Irish Centre on St. Patrick's Day, 1984. Effectively "on home soil", Pogue Mahone handed in the sort of set they would become famous for in years to come – a cantankerous blend of whiskey driven traditionals and freshly penned MacGowan tunes, the climax of the evening coming with a poignant, if decidedly shaky, rendition of 'And The Band Played Waltzing Matilda'. That the group were drunk and for the most part insensible mattered not. Their ability to drag a "hard-line crowd" away from the Centre's notoriously long bar (above which hung a portrait of murdered US President John Fitzgerald Kennedy) and onto the dance floor bode extremely well for the future.

Perhaps sensing their moment had come, the band decided to release independently a single, 'Dark Streets Of London', on their own Pogue Mahone imprint in May, 1984. Written by Shane, 'Dark Streets . . .' owed a clear musical debt to The Dubliners in terms of execution and pace, yet it was the song's haunting lyrical content that really grabbed one by the scruff of the neck. Instead of churning out hackneyed images of green fields and black-eyed colleens, MacGowan was instead telling tales of drunken tramps, ducking in and out of betting shop doorways in an effort to avoid the cold. "Now the winter comes down, and I can't stand the chill," he roared over a stirring back-beat, "I haven't got a penny to wander the dark streets of London . . ." In truth, it was the first indication that Shane was edging ever closer to the reality of "punk Ceilidh" – a sound that took its inspiration from across the Irish sea, but welded it to stories of a city full of winos, addicts and wizened old men teetering on the edge of collapse.

Stark, tuneful and bloody grim in places, 'Dark Streets Of London' caught the attention of Radio One DJ Mike Read, who began to feature the single on his breakfast show. However, when it was pointed out to him what Pogue Mahone actually meant, Read had little alternative but to remove the song from his play-list. Having already taken considerable flack for banning Frankie Goes To Hollywood's sexually charged début single, 'Relax' (a move which made Read seem both priggish and uncool yet, predictably, pushed the band to number one), he simply couldn't afford to court any further controversy. Now alerted to the dangers of the phrase 'Pogue Mahone', the BBC followed suit, subsequently issuing an edict to all DJs that 'Dark Streets . . .' could be played only between the hours of 8 p.m. and midnight. "Apparently," wrote *NME*'s Sean O'Hagan, "(this is the time) when it is permissible to say "Kiss my arse" in a language no one understands anyway."

In the end, the shunting of 'Dark Streets Of London' towards the midnight hour did Pogue Mahone little harm. In fact, it may have done them the world of good. "Mike Read had been playing the single," Shane recalled, "but it was just after the time of 'Relax', so he was . . . er . . . rather sensitive. Still, it got us a lot of publicity and led to us being signed." Though a number of labels expressed definite interest in the group, it was actually Stiff Records that lured Pogue Mahone out of the pub long enough for them to sign on the dotted line.

Formed in 1976 by Jake Riveria (aka Andrew Jakeman, former road manager for pub rock icons Dr. Feelgood) and Dave Robinson (rock promoter and former manager of Brinsley Schwartz and Graham Parker And The Rumour) Stiff was originally set up on a measly £400 and operated from a "small lock-up" in London's Notting Hill. Using the slogan 'Today's Sound Today' – a novel spin on legendary Sixties producer Phil Spector's motif 'Tomorrow's Sound Today' – the label specialised in one-off deals with new wave artists such as Wreckless Eric and most famously, The Damned, whose 'New Rose' single officially marked the first time punk was captured on vinyl. As a small concern, Stiff could ensure that an act was signed, recorded and "in the shops" within the space of just two weeks, a fact they were justly proud of. "For far too long,"

Jake Riveria reasoned in 1977, "there's been a gap between the million quid advance and scuffling about in a cellar. There had to be a middle ground, and I believe Stiff is it."

Riveria was subsequently proved right. Stiff seemed to have an uncanny ability to attract future talent, releasing début singles by the likes of Nick Lowe ('So It Goes'), Richard Hell (the seminal punk anthem 'Blank Generation') and Motorhead ('White Line Fever'). By the end of 1977, Jake Riveria exited the rapidly growing label to take on Radar Records with another early Stiff signing, Elvis Costello, whom he managed. Now left in sole charge, Dave Robinson set about expanding the Stiff's artistic roster to include the likes of Ian Dury & The Blockheads and, crucially, Madness, who became Stiff's major cash cow until their departure from the label in June, 1984. Keen to find a viable replacement for "Great Britain's favourite band", Robinson hit the clubs in search of the next big thing. What he found was Pogue Mahone.

"The buzz around the business was, 'How can anyone sign this group?'" Robinson later confirmed. "They were so out of it, they couldn't even perform a gig from beginning to end. They were just the opposite of safe, but that was part of their appeal. They were fantastically exciting – whipping up a football crowd-type fervour in an audience. I remember watching them playing in a pub, and after three numbers they fell from the stage and never re-appeared. I thought, 'If this could be bottled, if this band could be coerced into performing a full gig, people would love it.'" The man given the thankless task of cajoling Pogue Mahone to do just that was Frank Murray, who would soon take over as manager from Stan Brennan, owner of Rocks Off Records and former manager of The Nips. Like Dave Robinson, Murray was an Irish native, who cut his teeth on the road with another legendary Celtic rock act, Thin Lizzy. When that band broke up in 1983, Murray sought out new pastures, eventually finding his niche with MacGowan's motley crew.

Suffice it to say, negotiations between Murray and Robinson went well, with the latter jokingly offering to sign the group to Stiff for half a crate of Guinness. However, when the laughter subsided, Robinson dropped his bombshell. Stiff Records would offer Pogue Mahone a contract, but only if they changed their name. "Just before we signed to Stiff," Shane later remembered, "they found out what the name meant, and that *really* fucked us." After several heated exchanges, a compromise was reached. Pogue Mahone became The Pogues and Robinson had his men. And woman.

As news spread of Stiff's latest acquisition throughout the record industry, the rock press duly went in search of a trend. With New Romanticism long past resuscitation, and no cult springing up to replace it, spotting "the next big thing" was now a matter of some importance for music journalists. Nonetheless, the UK circa 1984 offered slim pickings for trend hunters. Aside from a spirited, if ultimately doomed glam-rock revival led by Hanoi Rocks, Marionette and Chinchilla, other aspiring groups such as King, A Certain Ratio and Bronski Beat continued to fiddle with effects pedals and synthesiser settings in an effort to create music of enduring worth.

Certain critics noted there were bands on the circuit who at least shared something in common with The Pogues. The Boothill Foot Tappers, for instance (led by Shanne Bradley from MacGowan's old band, The Nips), were keen to stress their bluegrass credentials, even going as far as to include a square-dancing rendition of 'Pick A Bale Of Cotton' in their concert set. Elsewhere, the likes of The Shillelagh Sisters, Yip Yip Coyote and The Skiff Skats were also experimenting with country music, skiffle and Western Swing. When one added the authentic Rockabilly twang of The Polecats and Hackney Five-0, a slim case could be made for the onset of a "Country" revival in 1984. Indeed, several journalists tried precisely that, arguing The Pogues were at the forefront of the movement.

Realistically though, there was no real movement to lead.

Light years away from trad, swing, skiffle or straight-up country, The Pogues' unswerving dedication to Irish music, punk rock attitude and the strongest available whiskey made them "a band apart". Even if they wished to raise a "flag of convenience", or swear allegiance to the latest passing fad, it was quite beyond their capabilities to do so. "We're all about a good tune, good lyrics and a stomping beat," reasoned Jem Finer. "And we're honest," growled MacGowan. Evidently, if they were "going all the way", then the group would have to write their own ticket.

FOUR

Declaration

In the last week of October, 1984, The Pogues released their first album for Stiff Records, the quaintly titled *Red Roses For Me*. In essence, the LP was a faithful representation of the band's then live set – in other words, a shambolic, yet lively collection of classic Irish folk songs, clattering instrumentals and the odd MacGowan tune. On the whole, *Red Roses . . .* was no masterpiece. Nor indeed a disaster. Instead, it was best viewed as a declaration of intent, a calling card from one of the few British groups brave enough at the time to ignore the lure of synthetic pop in favour of a more traditional approach to making music.

The album itself began deceptively enough, with a gently plucked banjo and mellow, almost sleepy accordion stroking the listener's ear. However, within twenty seconds, a whistling, backwards echo cut away all sense of sweetness and The Pogues were up and running. The song – the Shane penned 'Transmetropolitan' – neatly encapsulated the group's peculiar charm for all to hear: an insistent, up-tempo thump from the rhythm section of Ranken and O'Riordan, a rousing melody courtesy of Finer and Fearnley, and on top, the gruff strains of MacGowan and Stacy hurling drink-assisted abuse at the BBC, the GLC, Whitehall and anything else that came to mind. This was a tune that while sounding essentially Irish, could also claim to have roots firmly planted in both punk and rockabilly. A rebel song, then: "It's not a rebel song in an Irish sense," Shane countered. "What it's saying is 'fuck everything'. That isn't the same as 'fuck so and so'."

The pace kept up with another MacGowan original, this time a heated instrumental christened 'The Battle Of Brisbane'. Owing a clear debt of gratitude to The Dubliners in terms of execution and pace, its polka-like jauntiness allowed The Pogues the freedom to indulge their musical skills, providing Spider in particular, with a chance to excel on both the tin whistle and beer tray. Yet, it was *Red Roses . . .*' third song that gave clear indication the group harboured ambitions other than "kicking the shit out of their instruments." By covering Brendan Behan's timeless ballad 'The Auld Triangle', The Pogues countered any nascent charges that they were all blood and thunder, with little or no understanding of subtlety or finesse. In fact, the band's treatment of Behan's hymn to the vagaries of prison life was truly inspired, handing MacGowan a spare, almost desolate backing track to mull over. Rising to the challenge, Shane's interpretation of Behan's words – sung in a wizened, strained style – was spot on, capturing all the pathos, boredom and dead-end humour of time spent at Her Majesty's Pleasure: "In the woman's prison, there are seventy women, and I wish it was with them that I did dwell. Then the auld triangle could go jingle jangle all along the banks of the Royal Canal."

The respite offered by 'The Auld Triangle' was brief. Seconds after the pianos and accordions ground to a bitter-sweet halt, the group were back in more familiar waters with 'Waxie's Gargle', a traditional tear-up enlisting a cast of drunks, long-suffering wives and an ill-advised trip to the Galway races to drive home its point. Rambunctious, and at times, lyrically incomprehensible, its breakneck pace was again emphasised by Spider's penchant for bashing a beer tray against his head to keep time. Of more enduring worth was 'Boys From The County Hell'. Another MacGowan original, with a melody recalling the galloping cowboy ballads cut by the likes of Slim Whitman in the late 1950s, 'Boys . . .' offered up a disquieting tale of a "bastard" landlord getting his come-uppance from a group of aggrieved patrons. Revelling in images of unremitting rain, petty greed and murderous retri-bution ("We'll eat your frigging entrails and we won't give a damn"), the song's ice-cold sentiments made for uneasy, if thoroughly compelling, listening.

Shane's next offering, 'Sea Shanty', served up more of the same, though this time, with a degree of humour added to the mix. Based on a conversation MacGowan had struck up with an ex-sailor at a Kings Cross bus stop (Shane was drinking cider, the seaman Carlsberg Special Brew), the song's lyric told of an old tar forever marooned in the city, with only the bawdy memories of a life on the waves to keep him warm. An off-kilter musical romp, made all the more pleasing by Andrew Ranken's mauling of his drum kit, Shane often joked that he owed half of the royalties accrued from 'Sea Shanty' to the elderly souse whose recollections he'd plundered.

Following a faithful reprise of the band's first single, 'Dark Streets Of London', The Pogues again upped the ante with two beautifully judged compositions – MacGowan's anthemic 'Streams Of Whiskey' and an irreverent cover of the Irish standard 'Poor Paddy'. In the case of 'Streams Of Whiskey', Shane really had written *the* perfect drinking song. Meeting his hero, Brendan Behan, in an alcohol-assisted dream, MacGowan shakes the Dublin bard's hand and asks the secret of his gift. The answer Behan offers forms the chorus of what would subsequently become one of The Pogues best-loved tunes: "I am going, I am going, any which way the wind may be blowing . . . where streams of whiskey are flowing." An able encapsulation of Shane's personal recipe for happiness, 'Streams Of Whiskey''s anarchic gusto remains as fresh as a proverbial daisy some two decades after it was recorded.

The same might also be said for the band's rousing treatment of 'Poor Paddy', a traditional air brought to prominence by The

Dubliners in the Sixties. Detailing the wretched lives of the men unfortunate enough to have earned their living from working the railroads of England and America, 'Poor Paddy''s dilemma echoed the sentiments of many an Irish labourer throughout the ages: "In 1844, I landed on the Liverpool shore, my belly was empty, my hands were raw, with working on the railway . . . I'm sick to my guts of the railway." It seemed that, even in death, the unknown trackman couldn't escape his earthly fate: "In 1847, Paddy was thinking of going to heaven, the old bugger was thinking of going to heaven . . . to work upon the railway . . ." Following on from this purple patch was always going to be difficult, but The Pogues gave it their best shot, ably covering 'Dingle Regatta' – an instrumental tribute to the annual festivities held in West Kerry's famous fishing town – and 'Greenland Whale Fisheries', yet another traditional melody made famous by The Dubliners: "We hoisted our colours to the mast," growled a nautically inclined MacGowan, "and for Greenland sailed away, brave boys, and for Greenland sailed away . . ." Like 'Poor Paddy' before it, '. . . Whale Fisheries'' lyric presented a world where men waged war with nature (this time represented by a great fish), only to fall foul of high seas, chill winds and thrashing leviathans.

With benefit of hindsight, *Red Roses . . .*' concluding tracks clearly pointed the way towards the dual territories The Pogues would subsequently explore throughout much of their recorded career: to wit, the Celtic/spaghetti-western inclined shin-kicker and the grand romantic ballad. Penned by Shane, 'Down In The Ground Where The Deadmen Go' was a wild confection of rattling spurs, manic banjos and banshee howls – a perfect soundtrack in fact, to any Sergio Leone film starring Clint Eastwood, Henry Fonda or Lee Van Cleef. Conversely, the album's final moment, 'Kitty', deliberately tugged at the heartstrings, with MacGowan providing an uncharacteristically gentle vocal telling of the doomed love between an Irish freedom fighter and the girl he leaves behind: "Far better to part, though it's hard to, than to rot in their prison away . . ." "It's a Fenian song, about the Fenian uprising," Shane told *Sounds'* Bill Black. "(It's about) a guy trying to do a runner." In fact, MacGowan had first become aware of 'Kitty' whilst still a child. A favourite song of his mother's, he regularly heard her sing it at family gatherings and local parties. "It's a beautiful melody . . . a fine, fine melody," he would later confirm.

All in all then, *Red Roses For Me* was a promising début, made especially notable by the fact that MacGowan's own compositions were as good – and in some cases, even better – than the folk melodies The Pogues had chosen to cover on the LP. In fact, such was the quality of Shane's songwriting in general, it was often difficult to tell if one were listening to an established Irish standard, or indeed, a newly penned MacGowan original. For this feat alone, he deserved the highest praise – a fact not lost on the music critics who reviewed *Red Roses For Me*: "From the strummed banjo and lilting accordion that preface roar-ing singalong 'Transmetropolitan'," wrote the *NME*'s Sean O'Hagan, "to the final, unidentified voice offering an unaccompanied 'diddley I di di' refrain, there exists a wealth of evidence that Shane MacGowan's faith in the power of positive drinking music has paid premiums. If you think (The Pogues) have rehabilitated a music that's been asleep for a while," O'Hagan sagely concluded, "you're dead wrong – on both counts. The music has never been away and The Pogues in all their irreverent 'seriousness' have taken it out on a limb, where it all started . . . where it belongs."

Sounds scribe Rose Rouse was equally effusive in her praise: "The Pogues cannot help themselves," Rouse stated, "they are irreverent by impulse, pissed by seven p.m. and winsome by default. *Red Roses For Me* is a satisfyingly impure, purposefully imperfect and totally irresistible collection of lasting resentment, rebellious roars, watery-eyed romance and uproarious jigs. Fortunately, 'Fuck You, we mean it' underlines every second generation Paddy punch. The populous of Kilburn will be impressed." It was left to *Melody Maker*'s Colin Irwin to place the proverbial cherry on top: "The Pogues are a shock to the system . . . never meant for anything as delicate as stereo equipment. Finesse and subtlety are not words in their vocabulary. Drums, bass whistle and accordion clash violently in the fast lane. Respectable folkies will be appalled, pop people will be obliterated. It all makes me dizzy and I love it. Everybody else can kiss my ass."

Of course, *Red Roses For Me* wasn't without its faults. The production of the LP (overseen by Stan Brennan) was dry and lifeless in places, resulting in some of The Pogues manic energy being siphoned off in the mixing process. Ironically, the group's efforts to retain their in-concert power was inadvertently responsible for another of the album's problems: in the rush to capture the intensity of performance, Shane and Spider's vocals occasionally veered off into chaos, rendering some finely tuned lyrical ideas imperceptible and, therefore, obsolete. Nonetheless, these were but minor faults in the grand scheme of things, and in consideration of The Pogues' relative infancy (the band had been together only 18 months or so when *Red Roses . . .* was recorded) easy enough to forgive.

What remained significant were the themes the band, and MacGowan in particular, had explored in the songs of *Red Roses For Me*. Of optimum importance was The Pogues eagerness to present themselves as able interpreters of traditional Irish music. They remained mindful, however, of their place within that tradition: "If anybody thinks we're doing pure Irish music, then they're way out of line," Shane later told journalist Barry McIlheney. "We've all got far too much respect for that type of music to even try and get close to it in terms of playing. What we're doing is much closer to a group like The Dubliners than somebody like, say, the late Seamus Ennis." Still on a learning curve, both instrumentally and lyrically, MacGowan was all too aware that The Pogues might be viewed by critics as little more than a novelty act, lacking the skills and, more importantly, the seriousness to do justice to Celtic Folk. Nonetheless, he remained defiant in the face of charges that the group were lampooning Ireland's musical heritage for a quick buck: "This was never meant to be a joke," he stated emphatically. "We love this type of music."

Shane also gave short shrift to the idea that The Pogues lacked the necessary ancestral links to perform Ceilidh music, with their second generation status somehow diluting the group's credibility: "I lived in Ireland when I was very young," he said at the time, "and so did a couple of the other members of the band. So I reckon we've got as much right to call ourselves Irish as anyone with an Irish accent." It was a fair point. After all, nobody questioned Eric Clapton or Peter Green's ability to play blues guitar, though the closest either of them had ventured to the Mississippi Delta when learning their chosen instrument was Surrey and London's East End respectively. Still, there was a critical minority who viewed The Pogues' saw-toothed take on Irish music as sacrilegious – a slap in the face to all serious minded enthusiasts and performers of the form. Before long, both factions would meet in less than ideal circumstances, leading to a flagrant, if highly amusing, battle of wills.

Another facet of *Red Roses For Me* that merited serious examination was the naked aggression present in MacGowan's lyrical stance. On songs such as 'Transmetropolitan', 'Sea Shanty', 'Down In The Ground Where The Dead Men Go' and the notorious 'Boys From The County Hell', Shane was busy painting verbal pictures of casual beatings, serial whoring and ruptured testicles, all witnessed by a shadowy troupe of junkies, pimps, prostitutes and drunks. Though one couldn't debate the penetrating gaze behind MacGowan's tales of street life, the sheer ardour of his descriptions might be seen by some as potentially exonerating violent behaviour. An avowed humanist, Shane was having none of it: "People don't understand aggression . . ." he later told the *NME*'s Sean O'Hagan, "Don't understand that to really understand peace, to be cool about peace, you have to understand violence . . . you have to control aggression."

In truth, MacGowan was simply using his own experiences (albeit at a heightened level) as grist for the poetic mill, chronicling what he saw around him in the same way as The Velvet Underground's Lou Reed had done over a decade before. It was also worth remembering that The Pogues were aligning themselves with, and drawing inspiration from, Irish traditional music – a genre that pulled few punches in its lyrical treatment of injustice, insurrection and violent deeds. "Irish songs," Shane once offered, "are about fighting, fucking and drinking. The important things in life." With this in mind, MacGowan's photo-realistic tales could be viewed as an updating of that tradition, the only difference being that he had transplanted the "fighting, fucking and drinking" to the streets of London – the city he'd grown up in.

Perhaps the stickiest hurdle The Pogues had to overcome though, was the question of political alignment, or more specifically, where they stood on "the Irish issue". By choosing to cover 'Kitty' – a 19th century song that expressed the viewpoint of an Irish seditionist – the band were opening themselves up to charges that they were sympathetic to the cause of republicanism, a political agenda that called for the abolition of British rule in Northern Ireland and a return to a 32 county, united Ireland. Given the violent history of conflict surrounding "the troubles", and the enduring unpopularity of paramilitary groups such as the IRA, any link established between The Pogues and Ireland's more rebellious factions might have disastrous results for the band, effectively killing off a promising musical career before it had even begun.

Honest to a fault, Shane and Spider faced the press: "Just because you sing Irish songs doesn't mean you have to side with one particular set of extremists," an aggrieved sounding Spider told *Sounds,* "I mean, I reckon the best song written about the current troubles is Phil Coulter's 'Town I Love So Well'. That song tackles the most important issue – the lives of ordinary people stuck in the middle of fanatics from both sides. And I don't feel we have the right to do songs like that because we're not local boys. I mean, I come from bloody Eastbourne! Shane has already been beaten up over this type of thing, which is really stupid because we have no truck with the terrorist stuff."

Like Stacy, MacGowan was taking no prisoners on the issue of political misrepresentation: "I'm not going to tell you I don't believe in a 32 county Irish Republic," he confessed, "but that's got nothing to do with The Pogues. Musically, we're playing an urban representation of a really brilliant form of music that has been ignored for too long. Lyrically, it's a form of humanism, expressing a belief in the right of every human being to lead a decent life, without anyone shitting down on them. And that goes the same for a Protestant Orangeman as it does for a Black in Soweto. We are not putting forward any big solution to the Irish problem, because the only people who do that are people who just don't think. Why add another facile statement," he concluded, "about something which I'm totally confused about, and everybody I know is totally confused about, including all the first generation Irish people that I know."

An LP full of bright ideas, devilish humour and a liberal smattering of controversy, *Red Roses For Me* made a brief appearance at number 89 in the UK charts on November 3, 1984, before disappearing again into the musical ether. If the group were disappointed with the relative lack of attention *Red Roses . . .* had received from the record buying public, it was worth remembering that they had some distinguished competition to contend with. In the same month that The Pogues foisted their charms upon the UK market, indie darlings The Smiths released *Hatful Of Hollow,* Frankie Goes To Hollywood set out their stall with *Welcome To The Pleasure Dome* and a pre-ironic U2 unleashed *The*

Unforgettable Fire. Yet, while MacGowan et al. held their collective tongues regarding the merits of Steven Morrissey and Holly Johnson, Spider Stacy couldn't be constrained in voicing his opinion of Ireland's second most famous export: "U2 are a rock band, and I really hate rock bands," Stacy scowled. "To me, U2 sound like what would have happened to William Blake had he been exposed to lead pollution as a young boy, and then been given an electric guitar on his fourteenth birthday." Brave words, only to be eaten with a requisite helping of humble pie, some three years later . . .

FIVE

The Bastard Breed

Until the release of their first album, *Red Roses For Me*, it was easy enough to dismiss The Pogues as a temporary blemish on the face of British pop – a stray dog, if you will – wandering haphazardly across the halls and stages of Great Britain, looking for a suitable place to relieve itself. Notable for their ramshackle live act, which included between-song bust-ups and an infuriating inability to stay in tune for more than three numbers at a time, the group were a throwback to the days of punk, where the less professional you appeared, the more the audience loved you. Or spat at you. When brass tacks were applied, it was the same thing, anyway . . .

But times had changed since punk's moment in the sun. By 1980, the UK had embraced the fey charms of futurism, and with it the subtle allure of the synthesiser. Artists such as Gary Numan, Japan and Visage popularised a new form of music, one dependant on glistening surfaces, where melody seeped in and out of the cracks, a bleep here, a whistle there. All very clever. All very modern. Yet lacking any real emotional centre. The second wave of synthesiser-friendly acts – The Human League, Soft Cell, ABC and Depeche Mode – were certainly less robotic than their immediate predecessors, but still utterly committed to the possibilities offered by "the new technology". In short, mid Eighties pop culture was in the midst of a love affair with digital sound, and The Pogues' utter refusal to have anything to do with it marked them out as a musical anachronism, trading on values and instrumentation that had long passed their sell-by date. Nonetheless, *Red Roses . . .* proved The Pogues had something that couldn't be crushed by the onslaught of synthesis. It was known in popular circles as talent.

By flying in the face of conventional wisdom and embracing a form of music considered by many to have little to do with the 20th century, The Pogues immediately set themselves apart from the herd – always a good thing to do in the watery fields of pop. Additionally, in Shane MacGowan, they had a songwriter of true worth, whose gift with lyric and melody would only grow with time. As importantly, MacGowan considered himself a man on a mission, albeit of a kamikaze nature: "I want to go all the way with this," he defiantly stated in 1984. "I want to be up there with all the other fuckers in the charts. I want to be around the other pop stars so I can kick seven shades of shit out of them in the hotel rooms." A meritable enough ambition perhaps, but one that would require both a strengthening of discipline on the live front and the seduction of an audience large enough to hoist Shane and The Pogues out of the clubs and into the nation's living rooms.

The battle for recognition began in earnest in the autumn of 1984, when The Pogues secured the position of opening act on Elvis Costello's latest nationwide tour. Both a beneficiary and survivor of the punk explosion, Costello had forged an admirable career path since reaching number 14 in the UK charts with the release of his début LP, *My Aim Is True,* in August, 1977. Originally perceived by the press as a nervy, new-wave answer to Bob Dylan, Elvis (real name: Declan McManus) soon shed ties with a terminally ill movement by unleashing a cannon of superbly melodic and increasingly acerbic singles and albums: the B-Movie thrills of 'Watching The Detectives', the castigating attack on the nation's airwaves that was 'Radio, Radio' and the acid-tinged 'Oliver's Army' all marked Costello out as a songwriter independent of genre or fad. By the time he recorded 1981's *Almost Blue* (in essence, a love letter to the country music he'd been brought up with as a child), Elvis was the subject of a *South Bank Show* TV special – the first sure sign that Great Britain's musical intelligentsia had embraced him as one of their own.

Of course, there had been the odd hiccup on the way. For instance, Costello had compromised the integrity of his own talent by making racist comments about legendary black performers James Brown and Ray Charles whilst on a tour of the USA in 1979. More than a little drunk at the time, his unfortunate outburst in an Ohio Holiday Inn riled the tempers of fellow bar guests Stephen Stills and Bonnie Bramlett so much that the latter brought matters to a head by punching the bespectacled one in his face. "It (brought) a silly argument to a quick end," a chastened Elvis later confirmed, "and it worked too . . ." However, a rapid succession of classic songs ('Accidents Will Happen', 'A Good Year For The Roses' and 'Everyday I Write The Book') had enabled him to ride out all controversy, and by 1984, Costello was a man basking in the glory of yet another Top 10 album (*Goodbye Cruel World*), and readying himself for a 'Best Of' compilation that would mark the end of one highly productive cycle and the advent of another. A comprehensive tour of the UK's more notable venues could only add to the sense of Elvis's celebration. And, of course, his bank balance . . .

In fact, the pairing of The Pogues and Costello made a great deal of sense, with synchronicities abounding on several different levels. To begin with, Elvis shared The Pogues' resolutely Celtic roots, his father Ross McManus being both an Irishman and former singer with the Joe Loss Orchestra, whose version of Eire's national anthem 'The Soldier Song' – written, incidentally, by Brendan Behan's mother – was always accorded a rousing reception when performed by the troupe on McManus' native soil. Additionally, Costello had begun his recorded career with Stiff Records, releasing his first two singles, 'Less Than Zero' and 'Alison' and début album, *My Aim Is True,* on the label, as well as appearing on the now infamous 'Live Stiffs' tour of October, 1977 with his backing band – The Attractions – and fellow Stiff signatories Nick Lowe, Wreckless Eric and Ian Dury & The Blockheads. Though Elvis had defected with Jake Riveria to recently established Warner Brothers subsidiary Radar Records soon after (leaving Dave Robinson sole responsibility for Stiff), his historical ties to the company ensured that The Pogues had a viable enough connection when approaching Costello about the tour.

From The Pogues' point of view, it was "a decent enough break". Not only were MacGowan and his cohorts afforded access to larger venues in which to ply their wares, but as importantly, a ready-made audience appreciative of "the art of good, earthy songwriting". If the group were to make a connection outside of their initial support structure, Costello's post-teen congregation was as good a place as any to start – far better, surely, than second billing to Eurythmics or A Flock Of Seagulls. With typical alacrity, Shane summed up the group's attitude towards the upcoming dates: "Yeah, I reckon it'll be good practice. After all, nobody gives a shit about the support act . . ." Kicking off at Brighton's Top Rank club on October 3, 1984 (some three weeks before *Reds Roses For Me* hit the shops), the Elvis Costello/Pogues double header made its way across the UK with stopoffs at London's Hammersmith Palais (8/10), Liverpool's Royal Court Theatre (19/10) and a return to London's Hammersmith Odeon (29/10) before grinding to a halt at Norwich U.E.A. on October 31.

Comprising some 26 dates in all, reviews for the tour were glowing, with The Pogues enjoying a verbal massage from many a rock critic: "A thrilling ride", "A kick up the arse we all need", "Don't miss this lot – they're real." Though the band were still a little rough around the edges, an in-concert balance was starting to become evident to fans and press alike.

For MacGowan, the improvement in stagecraft had almost metaphysical properties: "We are trying to reach that perfect state where we are pissed enough to play well and enjoy ourselves," he told *Sounds*, "but not so out of it that we don't know what we're doing." The Pogues had also charmed Costello – enough, at least, for him to consider taking on production duties for their next album.

Nonetheless, before such a collaboration could take place, The Pogues had a tour of their own to complete. Given the title 'Lock Up Your Drinks Cabinets', the jaunt comprised several club dates in support of *Red Roses*, including a riotous appearance at the now demolished Hammersmith Clarendon, on November 10, 1984. One of London's more intimate venues, the Clarendon's beer-soaked atmosphere and nicotine-stained walls suited The Pogues' foul-mouthed drinking music well, allowing numbers such as 'Streams Of Whiskey', crowd favourite 'Muirshin Durkin' and 'Dark Streets Of London' to engulf the audience – making them part of the band's on-stage reveries. At each turn, it was difficult to avoid comparisons with The Pogues' live energy and the original in-concert venom punk had displayed: "Well, me and Spider are both ex-punks from 1976," Shane concluded at the time, "so I suppose we retain that spirit. Only today, that spirit has been tempered with realism, or to be more accurate, drink."

Regardless (or perhaps because of) their rebellious demeanour, The Pogues were beginning to generate real heat by the time of 'Lock Up Your Drinks Cabinets' – their very name synonymous with a good night out. Like many before them, it was only a matter of time before the band outgrew their current surroundings, and moved on to headline halls and theatres in their own right. They had a taste of things to come at Brixton Academy on December 6 and 7 when they supported The Clash, led by Joe Strummer who would in time play an important role in The Pogues' story.

MacGowan, ever mindful of retaining the old frontier spirit

of punk, remained suspicious of what further success might bring. Yet, given his sense of ambition (driven in part, by the failure of his previous act, The Nips), and an enduring wish to see Irish music accorded the respect he felt it deserved, Shane kept any doubts regarding The Pogues' future to himself. Spider, on the other hand, had already formulated a policy for all future ascension: "Some people might think that as soon as we (grow too big for) The Hope And Anchor, we'll lose our appeal," he reasoned to *Sounds*, "but basically, we'll treat the bigger halls as one huge bar."

At the very beginning of their career in late 1982, The Pogues' live fanbase comprised various family members, girl-friends, old mates and the stray Nips fan "eager to see what Shane was getting up to these days". In fact, some of these early devotees were filmed for the closing scenes of the group's first "home-made" video, 'Streams Of Whiskey'. As noted, this tribe grew exponentially over the following 18 months to number hundreds in the London area, with equal representation in every UK city. The Elvis Costello support slot undoubtedly played a part in introducing new acolytes to The Pogues' cause, and when one factored in glowing LP and concert reviews, in addition to a fine on-going relationship with the music press, it was easy enough to see how MacGowan and his fellow revellers were poised to break into the big time. However, the crucial factor behind the band's rapid climb to notoriety was the incredible word of mouth they created amongst Great Britain's second generation Irish community.

From the late 1940s onward, thousands of young men and women left a financially ailing Ireland to seek work in the UK. Discovering a nation eager to rebuild itself following the war years, these financial pilgrims ingratiated themselves into British culture by taking up manual or semi-skilled work in the construction industry, on the railways and in nursing – liveli-hoods typically available to the immigrant class of any prosper-ous nation. Establishing themselves in the major cities –

London, Liverpool, Manchester, Birmingham and Glasgow – the post-war wave of Irish settlers soon began to raise families, and by the late Sixties, their children were being assimilated into England's educational system. However, like all immigrant groups, the Irish were keen to retain a sense of continuity with the land they had left behind. Second generation infants were often sent to Catholic schools and traditional dancing classes (no matter the distance involved), in the hope that priests, nuns and instructors of the jig might instil in these young minds the cultural mores of a country they knew only through their parents and the odd trip home on the ferry.

In the main, these "once-removed children" tended to embrace their heritage rather than reject it, the reasons embedded in antiquity, propinquity and good old-fashioned common sense. From a historical point of view, the Irish, like so many African and Asian immigrants, were not accorded the warmest welcome in the UK – the sign 'No Blacks, No Dogs, No Irish' a familiar enough sight to many young journeymen seeking accommodation in the nation's capital. Faced with such negativity, they had few choices but to seek out their own company, building little pockets of Eire in neighbourhoods such as Cricklewood, Kilburn and Dagenham. As the troubles in Northern Ireland intensified during the Seventies and the IRA took to bombing the British mainland to draw attention to their cause (with fatal consequences), suspicion of the UK-based Irish was rife. Indeed, provoking civil unrest on the mainland – anything that might cause trouble for the forces of British law and order – was a deliberate motivation of the bombing campaign. As a consequence, the community closed in on itself, with the result that children of Irish families tended to mingle with other sons and daughters of like-minded experience.

This was borne out from a geographical standpoint, with second generation Irish kids taking the same buses, tubes and trains to attend the same schools, social clubs and dances as their peers. More often than not, both education and festivity were linked to the church, with the local parish disco responsible for bringing together "the young ones". As these teenagers became adults, the disco was replaced by the pub or the dance hall, with clubs like Cricklewood's Galtimore and National Ballroom, and Holloway Road's Gresham providing opportunities for locals to mix with the latest batch of arrivals from the old sod. All in all then, the Irish had created a community of itself, for itself, to retain, protect and perpetuate an enduring link to the homeland. Of course, the establishment of a society within a society was not wholly exclusive to the Irish. Italians, Asians, Poles, Jamaicans and other ethnic minorities all took similar measures to ensure the retention of their cultural identity in the face of change. Indeed, many of these groups – thanks to their mutual link with Catholicism – found themselves thrust together for the first time in church schools throughout the UK.

And therein lay the problem. While it was noble enough of parents to instil the essence of what it was "to be Irish" in their children, these selfsame infants had to negotiate their way in a very different world, creating links with a new culture that would soon inform much of their adult experience – from the football teams they supported to the careers they pursued. Though they were genetically linked to the old country and steeped in its heritage, the second generation Irish were a race apart from those who preceded them, constantly modifying the values they had been taught in order to survive and prosper. There was also the burden of expectation to consider. The Irishmen who settled in Great Britain after the war were afforded few opportunities beyond the pick and the shovel to make their financial way. In short, they did not want to see their own follow them into a life of rising at dawn to break their backs in gravel pits and ditches. Instead, the hope for their children was full acclimatisation, equal opportunity and a future devoid of hammer and claw. All in all, it was quite a weight for your average London Irish Paddy to carry into Thatcher's Britain in 1984.

The Pogues, therefore, were a godsend to this 'second generation'. Here was a band that not only represented a vital, accessible link to ancestry and birthright but – equally importantly – comprised men and women drawn from their own ranks. They were not playing the academically inclined, gentrified, traditional Irish folk music of The Chieftains, nor were they banging on endlessly about politics or plight. Instead, The Pogues were using "the dirty music" of The Dubliners as their template, singing songs about "fighting, fucking and drinking" and, in so doing, allowing their audience to temporarily escape the challenge of cultural assimilation and revel in more simple pleasures. In a nutshell, The Pogues were a circus come to town, and Shane MacGowan was the ringmaster.

Nevertheless, MacGowan didn't see it quite that way. Though he was aware of his growing importance as 'leader of the tribe', it wasn't a role he particularly coveted. In fact, he didn't feel representative of anything in particular, seeing himself as simply a chronicler of his times – one eye turned towards the past for purposes of inspiration, perhaps, but the other more than keen to observe the present. Being Irish was one thing, but MacGowan was reluctant to be used as a figurehead for second generation orphans or anyone else. He was, however, fiercely protective of his fans, and keen to brush aside charges that they were little more than a pack of drunks out for a good time: "They're not loonies, our fans," Shane told journalist Andy Hurt. "They've got a lot of energy – put it that way. Some of them already knew about Irish folk music, some of them (already) knew the songs. They're not *all* second generation Irish or Scottish either . . ."

It was a fair point. While the majority of Pogues' fans may have been drawn from one section of Great Britain's cultural pick and mix, the group also enjoyed great support from old punks, students and "lovers, in general, of fine wines, music and a good, good time . . ." Too good a time, if reports were to be believed . . . "Our audience have been really fucking vilified worse than we have," said Spider Stacy, in defence. "They've been called yobs, morons, like it's an 'all boys' party. The fact is that our fans are capable of being the most incredible psychopaths . . . people who could do the whole place over in minutes. (But) we play to thousands of them and they love each other, we love them and they us. We are where they go when they *don't* want to fight, right?"

Stacy's impassioned defence of The Pogues' audience was seconded by fellow bandmate Jem Finer: "Most of the groups I've heard or seen lately have been profoundly depressing, and the atmosphere that surrounds them is quite dead. I think if anything, we're live and spontaneous. Drink is obviously something people take to in such an atmosphere of excitement. They just come along and do it. Besides, we're sponsored by Guinness . . ." In the end, it was down to one of that self-same audience to defend itself. Peerless comedian and long-time MacGowan supporter Kathy 'Waynetta' Burke summed up the particular charm of attending a Pogues concert circa 1984: "The Pogues gigs were the friendliest ones you could go to because the audience were always so happy and pissed . . ."

The next instalment of The Pogues' career (live or otherwise) came with the release of the band's fourth single, 'A Pair Of Brown Eyes', in March, 1985. A primer for their forthcoming second album, the song – again penned by MacGowan – was a deeply human meditation on the atrocities of the battlefield, where amidst all the carnage, the one thing worth remembering for an injured soldier was the sweetness of his lover's gaze: "I lay down on the ground, and the arms and legs of other men were scattered all around . . . and the only thing I could see were a pair of brown eyes that was looking at me." With its swaying instrumental background and bold,

memorable chorus, 'A Pair Of Brown Eyes' should have catapulted The Pogues into the Top Thirty. However, the single
stalled at number 71, a victim of poor radio airplay and a promotional video that fell foul of the censors due to its depiction
of The Pogues spitting on a poster of then Conservative prime
minister Margaret Thatcher. "We wouldn't have *really* (spat on
her)," Spider said at the time, "because we'd have got nicked.
Besides, I wouldn't want to stand that near to her anyway . . ."
Still, the shoot did introduce the band to director Alex Cox, a
mercurial talent who had hit big with his first feature film –
the weird and wonderful *Repo Man* – only a year before. "I
once said something kind about The Pogues," Alex later
joked. "And their enterprising manager, Mr Frank Murray,
hunted me down. He gave me loads of 'Poguesware' – T-shirts,
tie pins . . . in fact I had so much of the stuff, I (started selling
it) down the Kings Road for a good price! In the end I did a
video for 'A Pair Of Brown Eyes' as a favour . . ." Enjoying each
other's company, The Pogues and Cox would soon collaborate
again, with different, if equally disastrous results.

Unbowed by the relative failure of '. . . Brown Eyes', the
band were back in the charts again three months later with
'Sally MacLennane', a good-natured, drunken cavort telling of
a musician's escape from – and eventual return to – the pub in
which he learned his trade. Inevitably, some had come, some
had gone, but the taps kept flowing: "So buy me beer and
whiskey, 'cos I'm going far away . . . returning when I can, to
the greatest little boozer and Sally MacLennane." In stark
contrast to The Pogues' previous single, which drew on states
of bitterness and longing to make its emotional point,
MacGowan's latest tale was more capricious, revelling in the
certainty of small lives lived out in great style. Arriving in shops
in the form of a shamrock-shaped disc and backed by a seductive rendition of 'The Wild Rover', 'Sally MacLennane' almost
put The Pogues "over the top", reaching a creditable number
51 on June 22, 1985. As with many a group on the cusp of

stardom, it was now only a matter of time before the bank opened for business. Shane, for one, was ready to spend, spend, spend: "I've been famous since I was 18," he cackled. "The only difference now is that I've got enough money to get pissed all the time . . ."

Unfortunately, all sense of celebration was temporarily put on hold when The Pogues finally made it to Ireland under their own steam to play a slot at the Cibàl Arts Festival in Kenmare, County Cork. Ostensibly, the band's first real stab at the Irish market (though they had appeared in both Dublin and Belfast as part of the Elvis Costello tour), the Cibàl gig and supporting promotional activity should have alerted Eire's populace to a new and exciting take on their own brand of traditional music. However, critical reaction to Shane and his cohorts ranged from bemused smiles to horrified glances with only the few who caught them in concert understanding their undoubted potential. In truth, from the group's first televised appearance on Gay Byrne's *Late Late Show*, a small – but extremely vocal – cabal of Irish pundits were openly suspicious of The Pogues. After all, here were the children of the ones lost to foreign shores returning home with a sound and representation of Ireland they would be glad never to see again.

To understand their attitude, it was necessary to look at how the country had changed over the past decade or so. Formerly defined as an agricultural realm, where only the privileged few gained employment with the civil service, Garda (police force) or post office, Ireland's entry into the EEC in the Seventies sowed the seeds of an economic rebirth that offered new hope to its citizens and, consequently, a steady reduction in levels of emigration. Aided by generous subsidies from the European community and the interest of American companies such as Ford, Ireland was busy rebuilding itself following centuries of internal strife, economic hardship and the mass exodus of its youth into a lean and commercially hungry republic whose future lay in international commerce and manufacturing. Once accused by Dublin novelist/playwright James Joyce of being "the pig that ate its own farrow", the Ireland of the Eighties was now capable not only of feeding its young, but ensuring they dined out in the best restaurants.

With the renewed identity came a wish to sever links with the more embarrassing aspects of the nation's character – in particular, the almost simian image Irishmen had acquired overseas. Though the likes of Oscar Wilde, W.B. Yeats, George Bernard Shaw and Eugene O'Neill had generated much interest and admiration in Eire's artistic heritage, the popular perception of the drunken paddy offering the pub out on a Friday night was one that refused to die easily. Keen to be rid of these meddlesome cultural ambassadors forever, Ireland's critical elite were now busy painting a more agreeable, genteel and, indeed, self-contained portrait of the homeland, in preparation for the time when it could fully reclaim its previous title: "Ireland – the nation of saints and scholars."

Into this cultural identity crisis came The Pogues, led by "a snaggle-toothed, jug-eared reprobate" who, to add insult to injury, was arguably the finest tunesmith Irish genes had produced in the last 100 years. Ignoring any notion of cultural rebirth or, indeed, the earnest pleasures offered by recent homegrown acts such as U2 and Clannad, MacGowan was busy erecting lyrical monuments to the very same drunks, labourers and violent melancholics that Ireland was so eager to forget. For Shane, there was no past to escape or deny – only a rich history to be championed in word and song. Nonetheless, for some critics, such a stance smacked of intellectual innocence, or worse still, "a blind embracing of traditionalism" that simultaneously "insulted its intrinsic backwardness". The whole matter came to an ugly head on B.P. Fallon's nationwide radio show where The Pogues were lambasted in person for their folly by a panel of Irish rock journalists and traditional musicians. Given the degree of enmity foisted upon them, it was hard not to feel sympathy for the band. Yet, there were some uncomfortable truths among the insults.

For one, Ireland had moved on. In order to survive the weight of its past and look the future square in the eye, it had to. Too long a victim of circumstance and oppression (both internal and external), the country's current upward trajectory could easily be compromised by a return to the black-eyed pessimism that had plagued previous attempts at financial and civic rejuvenation. To sustain this latest effort – and build upon it – meant shedding several layers of skin and exposing the cultural bones of the nation to contemporary influence. Tradition, however important in sustaining the Celtic soul, offered little in terms of forward momentum. In fact, for many, clutching onto the old ways was the very thing that had held Ireland back for so long. To certain critics then, The Pogues' reactivation of "the dirty song" was both a threat to the future and, at best, a back-handed compliment to the past.

Ultimately, such critical harping did The Pogues little harm. "Ireland's bastard breed" they may well have been, but the band were nonetheless accorded a warm reception at the Cibàl Arts Festival, and subsequently, began to pick up a groundswell of real support throughout Eire – particularly from the nation's youth, who were as excited by the group's novel representation of traditional song as their overseas cousins. Within the space of two years, not only would The Pogues become as popular as many of Ireland's homegrown acts, headlining huge venues such as the Dublin Point, but also receive the honour of whole TV shows devoted to them, such as RTE's *The Session*, where they performed without interruption for the best part of an hour. Inevitably, The Pogues' acceptance by the Irish came down to two things: their God-given ability to do musical justice to "the old songs" and, as importantly, MacGowan's enduring gift for coming up with "a few new ones". As the years went by, Shane began to see the funny side of the critical jibes that started it all: "Yeah, we started out in the fucking 18th century with The Pogues first album," he laughed, "then the 19th century with the second LP. (But) we got up to the 1950s with the third one!"

SIX

The Bounty Was Rich . . .

Following a return to England in July to perform at the Cambridge Folk Festival and the "Concert for Nicaragua" (held at London's Brixton Academy), The Pogues' second album – *Rum, Sodomy And The Lash* – was finally released on 17 August, 1985. A quantum leap forward from *Red Roses For Me* in terms of sophistication, production values and musical penmanship, *Rum . . .* was perhaps best viewed as a tribute from Shane MacGowan to the feckless, the transient and the irredeemably violent souls that wandered the streets of London, Frankfurt, Madrid and beyond. Without belittling the strength of later achievements, the LP also remains the pinnacle of MacGowan and The Pogues' recorded career.

Of the tracks presented, there were several obvious highlights. 'A Pair Of Brown Eyes' and 'Sally MacLennane', for instance, proved The Pogues' collective mastery of both the ballad and the rabble-rouser – the choice made to release these songs as singles indicative of a wish on the group's part to translate their new-found musical versatility into hard sales. With 'Wild Cats Of Kilkenny', a strident instrumental written by MacGowan and Jem Finer, the emphasis shifted again, allowing individual musicians to come to the fore with Jem, Spider and Andrew all displaying a new degree of proficiency and confidence. 'I'm A Man You Don't Meet Every Day' brought Cait O'Riordan into the spotlight, her soft, keening voice adding unexpected gentility to a traditional air recalling the drunken boasts of a Jacobite soldier to a crowded bar: "I have acres of land, I have men at command, I always have a shilling to spare, so be easy and free when you drink with me, I'm a man you don't meet every day . . ."

Two more traditional melodies, 'The Gentleman Soldier' and 'Jesse James' added elements of humour and betrayal to *Rum, Sodomy And The Lash.* In the case of '. . . Soldier', a naive young woman becomes the victim of a squaddie's lust, paying a high price for her physical surrender: "When nine months had been gone, the poor girl she brought shame, she had a little militia boy and she didn't know his name . . ." Shane's explanation of the song was curt, yet curiously effective: "It's about a soldier fucking an Irish colleen in a sentry box." 'Jesse James', on the other hand, saw the famous outlaw of the American West resurrected as a latter-day Robin Hood: "He stole from the rich and gave to the poor, he'd a hand, and a heart and a brain . . ." Unfortunately for poor Jesse, he didn't have eyes in the back of his head: "Well, it was Robert Ford . . . who shot him the back while he hung a picture on the wall . . ."

Of MacGowan's other contributions to the LP, both 'The Sick Bed Of Cuchulainn' and 'Billy's Bones' used images of racism, perpetual drunkenness and sickening violence to major dramatic effect, with Shane's lyrics basking in an air of casual, yet frightening authenticity: "Frank Ryan brought you whiskey in a brothel in Madrid," MacGowan howled over a stirring backbeat, "And you decked some fucking blackshirt who was cursing all the yids." "(Sick Bed)'s about an old geezer who's dying," he later told *NME.* "He's not a dosser but he's on his own, a bit pissed up, you know. (He's thinking) about all the things he's done this century." It was a rum list too – from catching syphilis in Cologne to kicking out the windows of any pub that declined his custom. 'Billy's Bones' was equally stirring in its evocation of uncontrolled rage, though this time, Shane's unlikely hero wore the uniform of "the peacekeeping force, 'cause he liked a bloody good fight of course . . ." Careering across the Middle East, machine gun in hand, Billy's end came not from the crack of a sniper's rifle, but after too good a time "on the Lebanon line . . ."

In the end, *Rum, Sodomy And The Lash* was defined by two towering compositions, one a MacGowan original, the other an old dance-hall tune whose harrowing message concerning the folly of war had been all but lost over the years. Dealing with the latter first, The Pogues' poignant rendition of Eric Bogle's 'The Band Played Waltzing Matilda' brought into sharp focus the reality of an Australian soldier's life – from a carefree existence in the outback to the battlefields of Gallipoli, where his legs are torn off by a Turkish mortar shell: "And I when I awoke in my hospital bed, and saw what it had done, Christ, I wished I was dead . . . for I'll go no more waltzing Matilda . . ." A tune that "had been allowed to cook" in concert for some time, '. . . Waltzing Matilda's inclusion on *Rum, Sodomy And The Lash* was proof positive that The Pogues could elicit as much pain and passion from three, spare chords as the finest bluesman or traditional artist.

Yet it was Shane's own 'The Old Main Drag' that caused the hairs on the back of the neck to rise. Based on his observations of rent boys trawling Piccadilly Circus and Leicester Square for custom in the late Seventies, the song didn't so much elicit an image of wasted lives and spiralling degradation as drag the listener kicking and screaming onto the very streets MacGowan described. In fact, as Shane's wretched creation descended further and further into a life of prostitution and drug abuse, police beatings, and finally, utter defeat, the wish to intervene became almost overpowering: "And now I am lying here, I had too much booze, I've been spat on and shat on, raped and abused . . . I know I am dying, and I wish I could beg for some money to take me from the old main drag . . ." " '. . . Drag's about a young kid who ends up on the skids," he confirmed, "the Piccadilly scene in the late Seventies, you know? It really hasn't got any hope in it." Listening to the ungodly drones that signal the end of the song, it's hard to disagree with MacGowan's assessment . . .

Making good on his original offer, the man behind the production desk for *Rum, Sodomy And The Lash* was none other than Elvis Costello who, unlike those before him, seemed capable of harnessing The Pogues' live energy and capturing it on tape. Ably assisted by engineers (and Pogues associates) Nick Robbins and Paul Scully, Costello also managed to excise many of the band's previous bad habits, with MacGowan in particular benefiting from the tightened regime. Instead of his lyrics being audibly lost to over-enthusiasm or "line-stacking", each word, syllable and subtle nuance now shot from the speakers with pin-point clarity. Additionally, months of hard graft in the clubs, pubs and halls of the UK had turned The Pogues into the musical equivalent of a swat-team – with band members watching each other's backs in case of trouble, and on occasion, handing the reins over to a particular soloist for the all-important "head shot" – be it a quick blast of the penny whistle or a lilting accordion break. Another secret weapon in their arsenal was the acquisition of Tommy Keane, Henry Benagh and Dick Cuthell on Uileann pipes, fiddle and horns respectively. By adding these instrumentalists to the mix, songs such as '. . . Waltzing Matilda' took on a new dimension, giving The Pogues' sound an air of majesty and occasional grandeur. In the years to come, MacGowan and his colleagues would build on this new found flair for arrangement, often with dazzling results.

Rum, Sodomy And The Lash's final triumph was undoubtedly the sleeve that housed the LP. In a fit of divine inspiration, Pogues manager Frank Murray came up with the idea of superimposing the band's individual heads onto the bodies of sailors detailed in an oil painting – *Le Radeau De La Medusa*, or Raft Of The Medusa – by 19th century artist J.L.A. Gericault. The resulting image of O'Riordan, Finer, Fearnley and MacGowan (wearing sunglasses, no less) staring out to sea from a ship-wrecked hull was both as funny and black as the title of the album – a phrase coined, incidentally, by Conservative Prime Minister and original "British Bulldog", Sir Winston Churchill – who used it to describe the foibles of the Royal Navy. Andrew Ranken, however, could take sole credit for liberating Churchill's comment from its comical origins and applying it to The Pogues' sophomore effort: "It just seemed to sum up life in the band . . ." said the drummer.

Crashing in at number 13 on the UK charts the week after its release (and staying around for a further 14 weeks in the Top 100), *Rum, Sodomy And The Lash* made stars of The Pogues, as well as finally putting a sizeable amount of cash into their bank accounts. A rare gem of an album, its many charms were not lost upon the critics, who lavished praise upon every single note sounded: "The Pogues hint here at two centuries of folk tradition," said *Sounds*' Jane Simon, "from the convict ships with their cargo of the first wild colonial boys saying fare-well to Old England (and Ireland forever) to Shane's pictur-esque young dossers of 'The Old Main Drag'. A beautifully rounded and executed album – and the whistle playing is spot on throughout." *NME*'s David Quantick was also a fan, sin-gling out Shane's contribution to the LP as critically impor-tant: "Shane MacGowan is one of our few *songwriters*," he enthused, "(and) a Pogues tune, for all its' rowdiness, is always certain to contain a striking, powerful, intelligent lyric . . . *Rum, Sodomy And The Lash* is more than the best record they could be expected to make at this time. It's more than a bril-liant example of a band using its resources in an imaginative manner. It's probably the best LP of 1985." In a year that saw the release of Kate Bush's *Hounds Of Love*, The Smiths' *Meat Is Murder* and Tears For Fears' *Songs From The Big Chair*, this was no small compliment.

Riding high in the charts, and with the critics on their side, The Pogues took to the road in support of *Rum, Sodomy And The*

Lash. Beginning their twelve-fisted assault on British audiences at the Scunthorpe Free Festival on September 1, 1985, the band wandered across the country (and Irish sea) with various dates at Dublin's SFX club (6/9), Edinburgh's Coasters (9/9), Aberdeen's Ritzy Theatre (10/9), Bristol's Studio (15/9) and Manchester's legendary Hacienda (18/9) before finally returning to London for a sold-out appearance at the Hammersmith Palais (22/9). In amongst all this activity, Stiff Records managed to sneak out another single from *Rum . . .*, the rather wonderful 'Dirty Old Town'.

Originally written and recorded by British folk giant Ewan MacColl (more of him later), the tune came to The Pogues' attention via The Dubliners, who regularly performed it in concert throughout the Sixties and Seventies. Like many of MacGowan's own creations, 'Dirty Old Town' was a romantic-sounding ballad hiding a hand grenade in the lyrics. On one level, it played out as a standard love song, with a young blade kissing his girl "by the factory wall" as clouds passed in the night sky. Yet, as the tale progressed, far darker images abounded: "I'm going to make me a big, sharp axe . . . I'll chop you down like an old dead tree . . ." Inspired by MacColl's youthful experiences in Manchester's Salford district, and featuring a cracking little harmonica solo from Andrew Ranken, 'Dirty Old Town' took The Pogues to number 62 in the charts on September 14, 1985. By which time, they had a new band member: one Philip Chevron.

Shane MacGowan had known Phil Chevron (born June 17, 1957) for some time before he joined The Pogues. In fact, MacGowan saw Chevron's group, Radiators From Space, many a time back in the good old days of punk. From their first single, 1977's 'Television Screen', The Radiators (as they came to be known) were regarded by the music press as "a tuneful, and at times, innovative spin on the sound of new wave", or as one critic put it, "Ireland's answer to XTC." However, despite a few good tunes – 'Teenager In Love', 'Million Dollar Hero'

and the aptly titled 'Psychotic Reaction' – and a fair to mid-
dling album (1979's *Ghost Town*), the band never really got a
foothold with audiences, and disbanded in 1981 – leaving
Chevron high, dry and somewhat depressed in his hometown
of Dublin. Due to various legal wrangles resulting from The
Radiators' split, Phil ended up working in a record shop for
the next four years, until Shane came to his rescue.

MacGowan's offer was simple enough. Jem Finer's wife was
pregnant and the banjo player wanted to take "maternity
leave". Therefore, there was "a space in the ranks that needed
filling". At first, Chevron was sceptical. After all, given the
failure of his previous group and the legal minefield it generated, a return to the stage was the last thing on his mind. Yet,
"Shane's songs . . . seduced me back into doing it," he later
confirmed. A good thing too, as Phil Chevron would bring
much to The Pogues, including truly bizarre dress sense,
manic on-stage energy and an intense style of guitar playing.
Following a brief probationary period that included production duties on 'A Pistol For Paddy Garcia', the splendid instrumental B-side of 'Dirty Old Town', Chevron became a full-time
member of the ensemble, even holding his ground when
Finer returned to the ranks. As usual, it was left to MacGowan
to sum up his new recruit's particular appeal: "Phil knows what
he's doing . . ."

However, the group that Chevron found himself joining was
facing fundamental change, thanks in large part to the public's burgeoning fascination with Shane MacGowan. At the
beginning of their career, The Pogues were eager to represent
themselves as a five man, one woman musical collective, whose
sole purpose in life was to bring traditional Irish folk out of
the pubs and lock-ins and back into the charts. In this goal,
they succeeded admirably. And behind the scenes, the group
was still blessed with a hive mentality – no leaders, no prima
donnas, just simple 'democracy in action'. Nonetheless, both
press and audience interest was now starting to focus solely in

Shane's direction, which both flattered and embarrassed him in equal measure. The reasons for such devotion were simple enough to understand. After all, MacGowan was The Pogues' frontman, the centre of in-concert festivities – and despite an occasional lapse into self-consciousness, he was really rather good at it: "(Shane) hates all the star thing, genuinely hates it. (Yet) he's still the most charismatic," Jem Finer explained. "You see that on stage – even when he's not doing anything, just ambling around, peoples' eyes follow him. He's quite a compulsive performer . . . a strange character. You just can't separate the artistic output from his character."

It was precisely this symbiosis of natural charisma and artistic sensibility that had so enchanted the UK critics. In his previous incarnation as Shane O'Hooligan – "face about town" – MacGowan was perceived by the press as a good-natured, if occasionally wayward, individual driven by an abiding love of punk. His tenure as leader of The Nipple Erectors did little to change that perception, the band's failure to capitalise on early critical interest temporarily consigning him to the 'Where are they now?' file. Yet, MacGowan's subsequent resurrection with The Pogues conclusively proved he was a songwriter of startling aptitude, capable of commercially re-invigorating an age-old art form. By fusing the sounds of his childhood with contemporary tales of London low-life, Shane had inadvertently set himself up as the natural, overseas successor to the great Irish poets and playwrights of days gone by – a fire-breathing, whiskey-drinking heir to the likes of Sean O'Casey, Flann O'Brien and Brendan Behan.

Still, despite an insatiable appetite for literature, an enviable knowledge of world history and an impressive ability to disseminate Epicureanism from Hedonism, MacGowan refused to assume the mantle of intellectual seer. Instead, when questioned about his gift, he offered the following pragmatic tips: "Look, there's a lot of shite talked about songwriting," he said. "It's a craft . . . just like any other craft. Once you can write a song you can churn them out or work at them. I work at them." The key, if there was one, lay in observation: "I write about what's happening around me," Shane explained, "rather than my own personal angst. What's going on (outside) is affecting me inside anyway. They're not separable." He continued: "Christy Moore once said that songs are floating around in the air all the time, melodies, phrases. And you've got to pluck them down out of the air – otherwise, they'll drift by and Paul Simon or some other bastard will get 'em. Mind you, he'd probably had a few when he said that . . ."

MacGowan was not above defending his ground, however – especially when confronted with theories regarding recurring lyrical motifs such as violence or mortality. When *NME*'s Danny Kelly raised the point that of the 12 songs presented on *Rum, Sodomy And The Lash,* nine carried images of death and destruction, Shane's response was downright pithy: "I could get all metaphysical here," he cackled, "but they're not really about death. 'Sick Bed Of Cúchulainn' and 'Sally MacLennane' are both about *returning* from the dead. (You see), the songs we do, (including) the traditional ones, confront, or rather, just mention death casually. There's no big fucking deal about it . . ."

In reality, Shane's resolutely anti-intellectual stance was wholly in keeping with the spirit of punk – a lifestyle and philosophy that scorned all analytical posturing, favouring instead the twin engines of emotional immediacy and perennial revolt. For him, the essence of true living was linked to American novelist William '*Naked Lunch*' Burrough's oft-quoted adage: "Exterminate all rational thought." By using drink, or anything else that came to hand, MacGowan could cut through all the cerebral "bullshit" and get on with the process of capturing the moment in song. He also had little interest in his public image: "I don't really care what people think of me," he once confessed to *Melody Maker.* "I don't have a great sense of my own importance, and that makes it difficult to deal with the bullshit involved in being a minor pop star . . . people thinking there's something special about you when there isn't."

Unfortunately for Shane, all available evidence pointed to the contrary. With creations such as 'The Old Main Drag', 'Streams Of Whiskey', 'A Pair Of Brown Eyes' and 'The Sick Bed Of Cúchulainn', he'd marked his card as a major songwriting talent – a viable, authentic alternative to the introspective miserableness of The Smiths' Morrissey and the overwhelming earnestness of U2's Bono. Escape from the responsibility of explaining his lyrics, actions or shoe-size was no longer an option. Like it or not, he was now public property. In typically obstinate fashion, he decided to abuse the privilege as and when he saw fit.

SEVEN

The Good, The Bad & The Very Ugly

If 1985 was the year Shane MacGowan and The Pogues achieved commercial lift-off, 1986 was the year they started paying for it. Like every other rock or pop act that broke the charts, The Pogues' work rate subsequently tripled in order to meet escalating public demand and capitalise on potential new markets. During a tortuous cycle of live appearances, press interviews and recording commitments, the band seldom saw daylight, except from the windows of a tour bus or through the cracks in drawn hotel room curtains. In the short term, such recognition must have seemed gratifying, but the eventual result of their extended moment in the sun was nothing short of horrific – their collective injuries reading like an extract from some medical journal on the effects of bio-chemical warfare.

Such maladies, however, were far from the mind as The Pogues headed overseas in January, 1986 for their first concerts on American soil. In essence, a short tour of the major hot-spots – no doubt set up in the hope of eliciting interest from the States' prominent Irish-American community – the dates proved notable if only from the point of view that Cait O'Riordan decided to "walk out" between shows in New York City, and was temporarily replaced by band roadie/tour manager Daryll Hunt. While the reasons for O'Riordan's dissatisfaction with the other members of the group remained "a matter for themselves", her overnight abdication was a portent for the future. During the recording of *Rum, Sodomy And The Lash*, O'Riordan had become romantically involved with its producer Elvis Costello (a situation Shane was not exactly over the moon about), and as things became progressively more serious between the two, Cait started questioning her long-term commitment to the group. Some five months after the New York wobble, the bass player's dilemma would permanently resolve itself, much to her satisfaction, if not MacGowan's . . .

In the meantime, The Pogues issued an EP, given the cunning title *Poguetry In Motion*. Presenting four songs in all, the release hinted at a broadening of the group's musical scope with opening track, 'A Rainy Night In Soho', more closely resembling the work of Van Morrison than The Dubliners or The Clancy Brothers. A gorgeous ballad, benefiting greatly from winsome brass interludes, 'Rainy Night . . .' found Shane at his most romantic yet, extolling the virtues of love, friendship and the emotional sustenance they brought: "I sang you all my sorrows," he cried, "you sang me all your joys . . ." 'London Girl' again saw MacGowan in devotional mode, though this time, the knives were out: "If you cut me . . . don't you think I feel?" Like 'Rainy Night . . .', 'London Girl' allowed The Pogues to explore new sonic territories, this time a clever fusion of Zydeco and Motown. But the band were soon back in more familiar waters with 'The Body Of An American', where "Yank" sentimentality clashed with Celtic whimsy at the funeral of Big Jim Dwyer, who "made his last trip to the home where his father's laid . . ." Featuring one of Shane's most acidic lyrics, 'Body . . .' drew stark attention to many an Irish-American's unrealistic expectations of their spiritual birthplace, a land where – according to MacGowan at least – their "Cadillacs" were stolen by the "Tinker boys" while they sipped whiskey with relatives. A fine collection of tunes, acting as an able stop-gap until the band had time to record their next album (it was to be a long wait), *Poguetry In Motion* finally pushed The Pogues into the UK Top Thirty, nestling in at a creditable number 29 in March, 1986.

Shane celebrated his appearance on *Top of The Pops* by getting hit by a taxi. The incident, which occurred on March 31, came at the end of an evening spent dining in Westbourne Grove in London's Notting Hill with old friend Alex Cox. After leaving the restaurant, MacGowan was clambering into the back of a car when a black cab struck him, throwing the singer high into the air before he fell unconscious on the pavement some yards away: "I remember going through the air," Shane later recalled to *Q*. "I flew across the road – that bit was pretty good . . . slow motion, like a Sam Peckinpah movie . . ." Unfortunately for MacGowan, when he woke up hours later in a hospital bed, the sensation wasn't as pleasant: "I'd broken my arm and torn the ligaments in my leg." In addition to the fracture and torn ligaments (which required an operation and setting in plaster), Shane also sustained severe cuts to his face. Though these would heal quickly enough, his knee needed major physiotherapy, meaning a protracted hospital stay was inevitable. As a result, The Pogues were forced to cancel a string of concerts in France and Germany.

Of course, the threat of physical injury wasn't new to MacGowan. Aside from the cut ear he received at a Clash gig all those years ago, Shane had been the recipient of several beatings from those taking exception to his political beliefs, punk clothing or lively habit of singing Irish rebel songs at the top of his voice in pubs. However, the closest he had come before to prematurely ending his run of cards surely occurred in the early Eighties, when an alsatian pulled his sleeping body from The Serpentine lake in London's Hyde Park: "I'd had a drink or two . . ." being his measured response at the time. Within 18 months of his accident in Westbourne Grove, MacGowan would again find himself in the wars, this time falling out of the back doors of a tour bus moving at fifty miles an hour. Miraculously, he escaped with only cuts and bruises. When one factored in a rapidly escalating drink habit and an inquisitive approach to all manner of pharmaceuticals, it was little wonder that the press were beginning to question his life expectancy. Perhaps sensing the publicity storms that lay ahead, Shane played down all queries regarding his health: "I'm all right," he said. "I've got a strong constitution. Others haven't."

Though MacGowan's casual dismissals concerning his well-being following the Westbourne Grove incident were credit-able enough (he was back on his feet in no time), music journalists were now starting to hone in on The Pogues' lifestyle – or more specifically, their continuing association with the demon drink. In the band's earliest interviews, they were content to champion a link between creativity and alcohol, conducting talks about their music and influences in the local boozer. Additionally, Shane's lyrical stance on songs such as 'Boys From The County Hell' and 'Streams Of Whiskey' made it patently ridiculous to deny the link between inspiration and alcohol. However, The Pogues' recent success had moved the goalposts somewhat. If they were to continue their rise to international stardom, the group would at some point have to 'cross over' – in other words, jettison their cult status – but not their cult following – and move into the artistic mainstream. Being regarded as a bunch of rowdy drunks might seriously hurt that ambition or, worse still, consign them to the musical fringe where critical plaudits often replaced hard sales. Simply put, to break the Top 10 – where the real money lay – empha-sis had to be deflected away from the pint pots.

As early as 1984, Jem Finer spotted the pitfalls of being 'The Pogues'. An intelligent man, Finer tried in vain to move atten-tion away from "the alcohol angle" and re-direct press cover-age elsewhere: "Too much has been made of this drink thing," he said at the time. By 1985, Pogues manager Frank Murray had joined the campaign. Sensing a media snow-job, Murray began an uphill struggle in damage limitation: "The group are at home in pubs (and) there's nothing wrong with that," he told *Sounds'* Andy Hurt. "Every group drinks, everyone goes to their local. It's just something the press have honed in on. You couldn't play to the public every night pissed out of your brains and still get off the pub circuit. The media just like the drinking angle. They've become obsessed by it."

Nonetheless, with press and public attention now firmly focused on Shane MacGowan, it was up to him to mount a defence against charges of perpetual drunkenness. And therein lay the problem. MacGowan and drink were inseparable – from the music and lyrics he wrote to the lifestyle he lived – one fed the other. Asking Shane to extol the virtues of clean living or publicly exorcise the devils found in a glass of whiskey was nothing short of emotional heresy, disingenuous in the extreme. Yet, in a supreme effort of will, he found a phrase he could live with when questioned about his levels of alcohol consumption: "None of your fucking business." A short verbal outburst, neither particularly clever nor funny, it nevertheless fended off most levels of journalist inquiry – for the time being at least . . .

Alcohol certainly wasn't off the agenda on May 16, 1986, when Cait O'Riordan finally tied the knot with Elvis Costello in a simple civic service held in Dublin. (It was Costello's second marriage, his first union – some years before – produced a son, whose mother Mary, trading on the Costello surname, became a radio DJ.) For Cait, matrimony signalled the beginning of the end of her career with The Pogues, and within months of leaving the band she secured alternative employment as an actress, making her film début in the independent Irish thriller, *The Courier*. Joining a cast that included established thespians Gabriel Byrne and Ian Bannen, O'Riordan's character – the winsome Colette – found herself involved with a vicious gang of horse-traders and drug dealers, all intent on murdering each other as quickly (and horribly) as possible. Though the picture was castigated on release for

81

its "frequent violence and often distressing realism", it still managed to pick up decent enough reviews, with first time directors Frank Deasy and Joe Lee and Cait herself all marked out for "great things". To no one's great surprise, *The Courier*'s musical score was provided by 'Declan Patrick MacManus' aka Elvis Costello.

MacGowan's eventual response to O'Riordan's marriage was to comically accuse her new husband of "stealing my fucking bass player". It was no secret, after all, that Shane admired Cait's talent, not only as a musician but also as a vocalist, and saw her as a significant part of The Pogues' collective armoury. She had also more than held her own as the sole woman in a group comprising five men, acquiring a reputation for speaking her mind as and when required. In fact, one of O'Riordan's more comical strengths was her ability to out-swear MacGowan, no mean feat when one consulted any of his lyric sheets: "(I'll) miss her female warmth and passion," Shane later concluded, "and her occasional viciousness and anger . . . she's quite a dynamic person, (but) I wish her well as an actress . . ."

The man given the eventual task of replacing Cait O'Riordan in The Pogues was Daryll Hunt. Born in Nottingham on May 4, 1960, Hunt was the son of a "fisherman with musical ambitions" who eventually ended up a member of O'Riordan's first group, Pride Of The Cross, in the early Eighties. After that outfit folded, Hunt followed Cait into The Pogues, finding work with the band's road crew. Still, stardom came calling in January 1986, when as we have noted, O'Riordan walked out between shows in New York, leaving Daryll to act as her on-stage substitute. Acquitting himself admirably, it came as no surprise when it was he who was offered a full-time position with the group following Cait's permanent departure in November, 1986. Known to be the "quiet, amiable type", Hunt's twin passions for both Nottingham Forest football club and Irish music were only superseded by his abilities as a bassist. Possessing a propulsive, fleet-fingered style, he would well suit The Pogues' future flirtations with rock and jazz stylings.

The day after O'Riordan and Costello made it official, The Pogues appeared in front of a crowd of 30,000 revellers at Dublin's RDS Showground as part of *Self Aid*, a project/gig designed to raise awareness of, and finances for, Ireland's unemployed. Modelled on Bob Geldof's triumphant *Live Aid* concert (staged on July 13, 1985), *Self Aid* initially took some criticism from the press for patronising the very people it sought to help, with accusations that the show "created a false impression of Eire's jobless," making them appear "incapable of looking after themselves" without the aid of rich rock stars. However, all carping ceased when it was announced *Self Aid* generated over 1,300 jobs, as well as £500,000 for those in most need. As pure entertainment, the event also worked well, bringing together some of Ireland's finest performers, including live sets from U2, Van Morrison, Christy Moore, Rory Gallagher, The Chieftains and a certain Elvis Costello.

The event peaked in the late evening when Thin Lizzy took the stage to perform a poignant reading of 'The Cowboy Song'. As the band's musical leader, the inimitable Phil Lynott, had died from heart failure following a drugs overdose only five months before, it was left to Bob Geldof to assume the role of frontman, overseeing a crowd stricken by a strange combination of exhilaration and grief. As usual, The Pogues received glowing notices for their set earlier in the day, though their placing on the bill between the gentle musings of Cactus World News and Chris Rea raised an eyebrow or two. Back in the UK, they continued their concert excursions with an appearance at Glastonbury on June 20, sharing the stage this time with Level 42, The Cure and The Housemartins. Given the gaping chasms between each bands' musical style, any hopes of a climactic all-star jam à la *Self Aid* remained unrealistic.

Away from the stage, The Pogues' next recorded effort

came as part of the soundtrack to Alex Cox's latest cinematic venture, *Sid And Nancy – Love Kills*. Detailing the doomed affair between Sex Pistol Sid Vicious and American groupie Nancy Spungen, Cox's film tracked the pair from Sid's fame with "Great Britain's most notorious group" to private squalor, wilful heroin abuse and finally, Spungen's alleged death at Vicious' hands in Room 100 of New York's Chelsea Hotel. Though the movie drew on the end days of punk for its atmospheric backdrop, *Sid And Nancy* . . . remained a love story at heart, with actors Gary Oldman and Chloe Webb bringing a shabby nobility to the principal characters. If the film had a message, however, it was surely "Love is not stronger than death . . ." The Pogues' contribution to this unconventional morality tale kicked off with Cait O'Riordan's 'Haunted', a sinewy little number decidedly more rock than folk in its musical leanings. Cait's swansong with the group, 'Haunted' reached number 42 in the charts when released as a single in August, 1986. Two other numbers, the hard-driving 'Hot Dogs With Everything' and sad-eyed instrumental 'Junk Theme' were also featured in the film.

For MacGowan, *Sid And Nancy* . . . fell well short of capturing the truth of punk, its hyper-realistic take on the movement's rise and fall seeming manufactured and unrealistic to him: "*Sid And Nancy* was crap," he later told RTE. "I was around for punk, and that movie didn't show it the way it was." Nonetheless, Shane had become firm friends with Alex Cox (a horrified witness to his experiment with oncoming traffic in Westbourne Grove), and their relationship soon found a new creative outlet in Southern Spain where filming for the director's next project took place in the autumn of 1986. Ever the maverick, Cox decided to follow up his personal love letter to 'the spirit of Sid' with a comical homage to the spaghetti western entitled *Straight To Hell*. Using the rocky terrain of the Sierra Nevada to re-create the look of movies such as *A Fistful Of Dollars* and *The Good, The Bad And The Ugly*, he assembled a number of proven actors – Dick Rude, Sy Richardson – and placed them alongside raw talents gleaned from the music industry, including ex-Clash frontman (and old pal) Joe Strummer and a pre-Kurt Cobain/Hole Courtney Love. In one of the most unfortunate casting mistakes of the late 20th century, Alex also decided that MacGowan and The Pogues were a perfect choice to portray the film's comedic anti-heroes, The McMahon Gang.

The result of Cox's endeavours was a sprawling, nonsensical mess that severely compromised one of the more promising careers in British cinema. Bereft of both wit and plot, the film seemed to wander from pillar to post in search of a suitable ending, which came, somewhat ironically, with its penultimate line: "Who's paying for this?" Critically slated on its release in 1987, finding a kind review for *Straight To Hell* remains an insurmountable task to this day: "Cox's Spanish quickie comes on like a snorter's rag revue and resembles the result of roadies bouncing ideas off each other after a gig," concluded *Time Out*. "With the exception of (leading actor) Sy Richardson, the cast are every bit as tall in the saddle as Arthur Askey in *Ramsbottom Rides Again*. As a parody of the spaghetti western, it is as witless . . . as The Young Ones' *A Fistful Of Travellers Cheques*, and longer, by Christ." Cox would ultimately survive the fiasco, going on to helm some truly interesting features such as *Walker* and the long underrated *Highway Patrolman*, yet *Straight To Hell* remains an abject lesson for all aspiring directors on how not to approach the business of making a film.

Ultimately, assessing MacGowan and The Pogues' contribution to *Straight To Hell* is as frustrating a task as actually watching the movie itself. Suffice it to say, they turn up occasionally, say their lines and wander off again – their overall performance conclusively proving they harboured little ambition or talent as actors. If there was a star in the ranks to be had, it was probably Spider Stacy, who as with his on-stage persona, could always be relied upon to deliver a witty quip or two. But, overall, Daniel Day Lewis had little reason to worry. "I think it was a good laugh," Shane later said of the movie. "It's real trash – that's what it's meant to be . . . an insane spaghetti western." Ever the philosopher, Jem Finer succinctly nailed the probable motives behind The Pogues' brush with cinematic greatness: "(It was) a bit of a laugh," the wise one confessed, "but at the end of the day, (*Straight To Hell*) deserves the obscurity for which it is destined." To add insult to injury, a proposed Pogues single from the film's soundtrack, 'The Good, The Bad And The Ugly', was subsequently shelved.

The group were considerably more successful in their next collaborative venture, which saw them team up with long-time heroes, The Dubliners, in the winter of 1986 to record a faithful version of that old traditional standard, 'The Irish Rover'. The seeds of the alliance were actually sewn several months earlier by Pogues manager, Frank Murray, when both bands met for the first time in – surprise, surprise – a bar: "I think it was in Vienna at some show or another," Dubliners vocalist Ronnie Drew confirmed to *RCD*. "We met in the bar and hit on the idea of a collaboration. But we'd also worked with (blues man) Rory Gallagher by then . . . so you know, you can't pigeonhole The Dubliners . . . we're too long in the tooth for that." One of Ireland's best loved acts, The Dubliners formed in 1962, experiencing almost immediate notoriety in their homeland for their raw, uncompromising take on Celtic folk. Eschewing all airs and graces, the group concentrated instead on perfecting the sound of the tavern – a roaring, good-natured music that ably reflected late-night lock-ins, exasperated barmaids and endless pints of stout: "We actually started out doing pretty straight folk," Drew remembered, "but as the Sixties went on, we loosened up a bit and that's when we became popular."

The Dubliners came to international prominence in April, 1967, when their single, 'Seven Drunken Nights', reached an impressive number seven in the UK Top Thirty. The LP from which it came, *A Drop Of The Hard Stuff*, fared even better, peaking at number five in the charts, and staying around for a further forty-one weeks. The USA soon beckoned, with the group appearing on the legendary *Ed Sullivan Show*. However, unlike The Beatles, The Rolling Stones and The Doors, who all shot to mega-stardom after their performances on America's most popular TV programme, The Dubliners drew a cooler response from Uncle Sam's children. "We wore suits," said Drew, "but we also had pretty long hair and beards (so) they didn't know what to make of us . . ." Slightly dulled by their experiences across the Atlantic, the act continued to fare well in England, notching up two further hit singles with 'Black Velvet Band' (originally recorded by the Kinsfolk Folk Group) and the imaginatively titled 'Maids, When You're Young, Never Wed An Old Man'. The albums *The Best Of The Dubliners, More Of The Hard Stuff* and *Drinkin' And Courtin'* were also successful, with Top Thirty placings for each. Nonetheless, by the end of the Sixties, their chart appeal in the UK started to dwindle, though live concerts remained well attended.

In Ireland, it was a different story, where over the years, The Dubliners were increasingly viewed as a national institution, or as one critic put it, "An always refreshing and honest example of Irish working-class music." Of course, there was the odd detractor or two, who saw the band's steadfast refusal to stray far from their traditional roots as evidence of creative paralysis. Yet, for Shane MacGowan, The Dubliners' ability to find endless inspiration in the "old songs, the dirty songs" was something to be championed. "'A Drop Of The Hard Stuff' . . . *Seven Drunken Nights* . . . (You see), the folk people (are) divided into two groups," he told Norway's *Beat* magazine. "The purists and the progressives, (and The Dubliners') folk music appealed to (the) 'no bullshit' people." As did the eventual result of The Pogues' team-up with Drew and his 'black velvet band'.

Taking the bones of one of Eire's best-loved songs and shaking them to sawdust, the fleet-fingered collective handed in a fine version of 'The Irish Rover', with Shane and Ronnie vocally trading the story of a boat destined to sink from the time it pulled out of port: "We had sailed seven years when the measles broke out and the ship lost its way in the fog," howled the pair, "And that whale of a crew was reduced down to two . . . just myself and the Captain's dog."

For MacGowan, The Pogues' collaboration with The Dubliners on 'The Irish Rover' was surely a dream come true – in fact, he appears genuinely humbled when standing next to Ronnie Drew in the promotional video for the song. Yet, Drew was equally complimentary of The Pogues' talent, seeing the group's energy and commitment as a way of keeping himself in the game. "When you've been doing it as long as we have, it's important to have variety," he confessed. "Working with The Pogues was great for that . . . it keeps you on your toes . . . keeps you interested." Released as a bold marker for The Dubliners' 25th anniversary celebrations in March, 1987, '. . . Irish Rover' hit number one in Ireland, and number eight in the UK – The Pogues first entry into the hallowed Top 10. Riding on a wave of new-found success and collective longevity, The Dubliners chanced their arm once again in Great Britain with *25 Years Celebration*, an LP that paraded their finest moments. Peaking at number 43, it was their first chart placement in the UK since 1968. Though he never stated as much, Shane had just repaid in kind a childhood debt.

Shane in 1985. (*David Corio/SIN*)

One of the many Nips line-ups, with Shane
on the far right.

Shane in 1984. (*Robin Barton/SIN*)

The Pogues in 1986, back row, left to right: Phil Chevron, Jem Finer, Cait O'Riordan, Andrew Fearnley;
front: Andrew Ranken, Shane, Spider Stacy. (*Rex*)

Shane at home in London, circa 1985. (*Iain McKell/Retna*)

Shane on stage at the time of *Rum Sodomy And The Lash*. (*Steve Double/SIN*)

The classic Pogues line-up of 1987, left to right: Daryll Hunt, Phil Chevron, Andrew Ranken, Terry Woods, Jem Finer, Andrew Fearnley, Spider Stacy and Shane. (*LFI*)

Shane on stage with Joe Strummer at the Electric Ballroom in Camden Town, November 17, 1987. (*Steve Double/SIN*)

Ronnie Drew of The Dubliners joins Shane and The Pogues
on stage at the Fleadh in Finsbury Park. (*Steve Double/SIN*)

Shane with Kirsty MacColl. (*LFI*)

Spider Stacy, Shane and Jem Finer in 1989. (*Steve Double/Retna*)

Shane with actor Matt Dillon during the shooting of the video for 'Fairytale Of New York' in 1987. (*LFI*)

Shane just before he and The Pogues parted company. (*Leo Regan/SIN*)

Actor Johnny Depp with Shane, uncharacteristically clutching a bottle of mineral water. (*Rex*)

Shane launches his solo career in the mid-Nineties. (*Martyn Goodacre/SIN*)

Shane in 1999, performing at an open-air concert in Guildford. (*LFI*)

EIGHT

A Year On The Tiles

If 1986 was the year of 'the concert hall, recording studio and celluloid disaster', then 1987 heralded little change, representing another 12 months of "relentless slog" and crippling hangovers. Averaging between 200 and 250 shows per annum, The Pogues practically lived on stage throughout the late Eighties, their reputation as one of the UK's best live acts ensuring packed houses from Aberdeen to Cornwall. "We represent the people who don't get the breaks," Phil Chevron stated. "People can look at us and say, 'My God, if that bunch of tumbledown wrecks can do it, so can I.' " Chevron's remarks were borne out by the almost symbiotic relationship between The Pogues and their fans, with audiences out-singing (or more accurately, out-shouting) the music pouring from the speakers.

For MacGowan, the crowd's enthusiasm often produced a restorative effect on his central nervous system. "If I'm in a really bad way, there's nothing that can save the gig," he later confessed. "Although with my audience – or the audiences I've played to – if they see I'm down, they're capable of bringing me up . . ." In the end, it was a simple matter of emotional economics. "People just like going out and having a good time," Shane told *Sounds*' Antonella Black. "I don't mean . . . posing in cafes . . . I mean actually going out and going bloody nuts. It's great getting pissed out of your head . . . draining yourself of every ounce of energy – that's why people take drugs, go to football matches, go to (our) pop concerts . . . it's about letting go."

To aid the audience in the process of "letting go", The Pogues had become consummate showmen, each band member accorded a particular on-stage role. In Jem Finer's case, the easiest analogy to draw was that of a dishevelled university professor, observing the revellers before him with a combination of bemused curiosity and obvious affection. Never one for the grand gesture, the closest Finer came to 'freaking out' was cracking a wry smile each time MacGowan missed a vocal cue. In stark contrast, James Fearnley seemed to view the stage as his own personal gymnasium. Soaked in sweat from song number one, Fearnley would have made a fine dustman, given his ability to throw the accordion from shoulder to shoulder like an errant bin. Like James, the rhythm section of Andrew Ranken and Daryll Hunt were men dedicated to the pursuit of in-concert circuit training, with smiles and grimaces punctuating each cymbal crash or flattened fifth. To their left was "the whirling Dervish", Phil Chevron – a man for whom the 'scissor kick' was surely invented. The clothes horse of the group, Chevron's penchant for silly hats and even sillier bow ties seldom detracted from a guitar style that swung between downright aggressive and "sheer bloody maniacal".

Then there were the frontmen. In Spider Stacy's case, a joke was seldom far away, his comedic gifts often equalling his prowess as an instrumentalist. Wandering the stage aimlessly – cigarette and penny-whistle alternating in terms of importance – Stacy could always be relied upon to raise a smile from the audience, or a thump from his fellow musicians. And in the midst of it all stood MacGowan, a protean blend of genuine shyness and sheer lunacy. Fags stuffed in his front pocket, beer bottle in hand, Shane was, in truth, as much a part of the crowd as he was the band – the only difference being that he was probably the reason they were all there in the first place.

Best summed up as a collective show of forearms – sleeves rolled up to do a night's work – The Pogues' raucous stage act was unique in the annals of folk. Long-time supporter and occasional pop star Billy Bragg understood this part of their appeal better than most. "Instead of coming at folk music like Steeleye Span or Fairport Convention, they got hold of it by the lapels and threw it down the stairs," he told the BBC. "Nobody had ever gone at it like that . . . like a bunch of navvies, if I might use that phrase. The Pogues were just really exciting – it was like punk, but *folk* music."

Strangely enough, the final recruit to The Pogues' cause had played a fundamental part in establishing the very movement MacGowan was now so actively manhandling. Born in Dublin on December 4, 1947, Terry Woods' résumé read like an extract from a *Who's Who* of folk music, his name inextricably linked to some of the best bands to emerge from the genre. Beginning his musical career in the late Sixties with Ireland's influential trio, Sweeney's Men, Woods soon found himself a charter member of the legendary Steeleye Span, alongside his wife Gay, Ashley 'Tyger' Hutchings (ex-Fairport Convention), Maddy Prior and Tim Hart. Named "after a Lincolnshire waggoner celebrated in song", Steeleye's subtle fusion of folk gentility and rock dynamics charmed critics from the off, their début LP, 1970's *Hark, The Village Wait* still regarded as a benchmark release three decades later. However, Woods became increasingly disenchanted with the direction the group were taking and soon sought fresh pastures: "I used to be in Steeleye Span," he later confirmed to *Q*, "when they were playing the sort of music you'd want to listen to . . ."

By 1971, Terry and Gay Woods were recording under their own name, with LPs such as *Backwoods* and 1976's criminally neglected *The Time Is Right* earning the couple a reputation as "mavericks at the adventurous end of folk rock". Nonetheless, despite a cult following throughout Great Britain and Europe, they subsequently lost their record deal with Polydor and found themselves back in Ireland. One last album, 1978's *Tenderhooks* (released by Dublin's Mulligan label) forever defined The Woods Band's plaintive appeal, but by then it was too little, too late. The pair duly separated, Gay finding a home with progressive rock act Auto De Fe and Terry retiring completely from the music business to work in a plastics factory in County Meath.

Salvation came for Woods in late 1986, when he was approached by old friend and Pogues manager Frank Murray about the possibility of joining "the boys". One could only admire Murray's combination of thoughtfulness and sheer business acumen. After all, here was one of Ireland's finest multi-instrumentalists languishing in relative obscurity, when he could be contributing his talents to the UK's premier folk-based outfit. Unsurprisingly, Terry took little persuading: "One of the reasons I wanted to join The Pogues was because I particularly liked the way they attacked Irish music. At that point in time (it) had gone into the doldrums again – become a kind of parlour music – and for me, it's not about that at all." A masterly player, Woods' command of the mandolin, banjo, concertina, bagpipes and cittern was fully absorbed into The Pogues' ranks in the summer of 1987 – by which time, he was already extolling the band's virtues in brisk fashion. "We know what we're fucking doing," he told *NME*. "The Pogues are slightly shambolic, (but) maybe that's the best way we can be. That's a natural thing. (It) seems to be the way this band works . . . a disordered order."

Though The Pogues' ranks now numbered seven in all, there was little chance of on-stage overcrowding. In fact, the band spent the warmer months of 1987 performing in expansive arenas and stadiums throughout Europe and the USA in support of the mighty U2. Arguably the biggest young rock band in the world at the time, U2's accession to the throne of rock'n'roll royalty occurred in March, 1987 with the release of their sixth album, *The Joshua Tree*. Achieving platinum status within seven days in the UK (235,000 copies sold), the LP sub-sequently went on to top the American charts, where it remained number one for nine weeks in all. When one factored in two hit singles, 'With Or Without You' and 'I Still Haven't Found What I'm Looking For', as well as blanket rotation of their videos on *MTV*, U2 were an unstoppable force, their only serious rivals – in sales terms, at least – being Dire Straits, who had recently sold over three million copies of their own masterwork, *Brothers In Arms*. For The Pogues then, the acquisition of a warm-up slot on the year's biggest tour was a fine opportunity to introduce their wares to a potentially lucrative new audience.

The pairing of U2 and The Pogues was a strange one, both in concert and on paper. In U2's case, their live shows were grandiose affairs, full of canny stage props, high musical drama and a frontman seeking emotional catharsis somewhere in the lighting rig. The Pogues, on the other hand, were the quintessential "little band that could", used to exchanging energy and spittle with an audience only inches away. No matter how successful they might become, part of The Pogues' intrinsic charm was their reticence to invoke the great rock god. Instead, they chose to dabble in earthier magic, summoning various folk demons with a heady potion of alcohol, sweat and ancient profanities. Putting aside this contrasting approach to the art of stagecraft, there was also the not insignificant matter of cultural representation to consider. U2 were shining ambassadors of the new Ireland, the group's global success emblematic of the nation's wish to lead rather than follow. The Pogues, conversely, were actively engaged in lionising Eire's past, their sound and message a throwback to times some were eager to excise from memory. In short, the differences between both groups were considerable.

Yet, if one kept digging, commonalties began to surface. Both Bono and Shane MacGowan, were masterful lyricists – the latest in a long line of Irishmen for whom words were almost sacred things. For Bono, inspiration was predominantly drawn from his own contemplation of faith, with U2 songs brimful of Judaic and Christian imagery. Shane's musings were, of course, habitually linked to the bottle, though historical events, bloody conflict and the harsh realities of street-life were also important to his work. In addition, though they approached showmanship in radically different ways, both frontmen could be relied upon to ignite a crowd, leading them to the point of physical and emotional exhaustion. Last but not least, there was the sheer depth of ambition exhibited by both bands. U2 wanted the world on their side – that much was obvious from the group's legendary (or infamous, depending on your point of view) appearance at Live Aid in 1985. But it was also worth remembering that The Pogues had fought hard to get their bite of the proverbial cherry. Having put folk music back into the UK charts, they were now being presented with an opportunity to conquer brand new territories – perhaps even steal the hearts and minds of a rock audience many thought would always elude them. MacGowan once said he wanted "to go all the way with this." Now was his chance.

The Pogues' introduction to the joys of stadium life began in earnest in July, 1987 at Dublin's Croke Park. Located in the north-east quarter of Eire's capital, Croke Park was a huge, imposing structure, capable of housing over 80,000 spectators. Home to both the Gaelic Athletic Association, and annual football and hurling finals, it was as representative of Irish sporting life as England's Wembley stadium was to fans of soccer. The fact that U2 had sold out the venue in a matter of hours spoke volumes about their popularity on native soil. With additional support coming from The Dubliners, the gig reminded MacGowan more of a church service than a rock'n' roll shindig: "I like U2, and I've got their records," he admitted to the *Sunday Tribune*, "but I wouldn't like to be (Bono). Too many people think he's God. I don't think it's affected him – I think he's pretty cool, you know? (And) I agree with (his) peace thing and that, but it's all . . . such a religious, spiritual, mystical thing. It was like being at an open-air mass. That's what struck me about Croke Park . . ."

Spiritual evocations aside, The Pogues benefited greatly from their temporary alliance with U2, gaining a critical foothold with both European and American audiences, as well as permanently impressing their in-concert hosts. In fact, over a decade later, Bono was still singing the praises of Shane MacGowan to anyone who might listen. "I don't think anyone writes better lyrics than Shane, " he told the BBC, "the words are everything for him – that's where he lives really." Sadly, U2's vocalist has yet to respond to Spider Stacy's youthful allegation that his band sounded like "William Blake, (if) he'd been exposed to lead pollution as a young boy, and then . . . given an electric guitar on his 14th birthday."

Keen to capitalise on the momentum gained by their recent stadium jaunt, The Pogues stayed on the road for much of the autumn, lining up a comprehensive tour of Ireland's ballrooms, as well as a short return to the USA and Canada in November, 1987. Here, the band co-headlined three weeks worth of club dates with Spanish-American roots-rockers Los Lobos, who had recently hit number one in The States with their version of 'La Bamba', the traditional Mexican wedding tune made famous by Fifties teenage idol (and original Latino rocker), Ritchie Valens. The song actually came from the soundtrack of *La Bamba – The Movie,* a spry, if occasionally romanticised account of Ritchie's brief but eventful life, to which Los Lobos contributed eight tracks in all – including, as luck would have it, 'C'mon Let's Go', another Valens composition which was riding high in the US charts as their concerts with The Pogues got underway.

Unfortunately, Pogues guitarist Phil Chevron wasn't part of the starting line-up, having recently succumbed to a particularly vicious stomach ulcer. "It reached a point when I felt so ill that I simply had to make time to do something about it, " he later told *Q*. "It was lucky I did it sooner rather than later . . . I would have got very ill otherwise." No doubt brought about by the excesses of road life, Chevron's complaint put The Pogues in a bit of a spot. However, a replacement was quickly found in the somewhat surprising form of ex-Clash frontman Joe Strummer. A long-time friend and supporter of the group, Strummer's fortunes had been decidedly mixed since winding up The Clash in November, 1985. Putting music on the back-burner for the time being, he elected to pursue a career in acting, first starring alongside The Pogues in Alex Cox's 1986 cinematic disaster *Straight To Hell*, before re-teaming with Cox a year later to film *Walker*, a compelling true story of an American adventurer who through a combination of sheer guile and military force, found himself elected President of Nicaragua in 1855.

Following his work on *Walker*, Joe actually spent some time with The Pogues, first performing a spirited version of his own 'London's Calling' alongside the group on Ireland's top-rated pop show, *The Session*, and then joining them for a "quick gig and a half" at London's Electric Ballroom. Therefore, he was already familiar with much of their live material. However, learning the songs note by note was a more difficult matter altogether. Legend has it that the group attempted to teach Strummer nearly two dozen songs in one 24 hour period, leaving him an exhausted heap in the corner. Yet he was, by his own admission, "All systems go" when the band finally took to the stage for the first date of their American tour on November 10, 1987. In the end, Joe's temporary assimilation into The Pogues' ranks went well, the band even paying him the compliment of including 'London's Calling' and that other hardy Clash perennial 'I Fought The Law' in their set.

For his part, Strummer heaped praise on his new-found chums: "Jem Finer's the Bill Wyman of The Pogues," he later confirmed. "Without him, they're all going to float away in the air." Spider Stacy was also singled out for a medal or two:

"Spider will never be short of a word," Joe laughed. "He's a great wit . . . the personality of the band." Inevitably, MacGowan took most honours: "Shane might be crazy, but he's also a genius," Strummer told the *NME*'s Steve Pyke. "You can put his work beside anyone you'd care to mention – Lou Reed, Brendan Behan, whoever . . ."

Though their camaraderie appeared for the most part genuine, there was still the odd press rumour circulating about behind the scenes rivalry between Joe and Shane. Both camps were eager to nip any such gossip in the bud. "If I come aboard, I don't want to elbow in on *anything*," Strummer stated emphatically. "I just want to do justice to (Shane's) songs. Anyway, I've known him and Spider vaguely for years. They were just two crazies from the punk days." Stacy clarified The Pogues' position: "I wish we could keep him," he said, "(but) obviously not at the expense of Philip. Because he's fitted in so well there must be a space that needs filling. If we had them together, then it would be perfect . . ." Regrettably, it wasn't to be. Following the tour, Chevron re-entered The Pogues' ranks and Joe returned to the movies, this time providing the musical score for director Marissa Silver's second feature, *Permanent Record*. Still, the seeds for future collaborations had been sown – some of which were to be intensely creative, others, simply tragic.

NINE

Sipping Champagne In The Drunk Tank

By the winter of 1987, The Pogues were well on their way to becoming one of Europe's premier live attractions. Nonetheless, the band hadn't actually released a new album since August, 1985. There had been the odd EP and single – *Poguetry In Motion* and 'Haunted' – plus a contribution to WOMAD's *Talking Book – An Introduction To Europe* LP, which saw The Pogues joining forces with the likes of Dick Gaughan, The Cocteau Twins and France's Ti Jazz. Yet, the group were conspicuous by their absence when it came to the UK charts. The explanation for the dearth of new recorded material was simple enough: Stiff Records were in the process of coming apart. After nearly a decade of success as one of England's largest (leading) independent labels, the late Eighties had seen a sharp decline in Stiff's fortunes, leaving a company that was once home to household names such as Madness, Elvis Costello and Ian Dury on the brink of financial bankruptcy. A shadow of its former self, Stiff's artistic roster at the end of 1987 comprised just two acts: The Mint Juleps and Furniture. While both bands surely had their merits, neither could be expected to turn the tides surrounding a rapidly sinking ship.

It came as no surprise then, when news was announced of Stiff Records impending "amalgamation" with another, more financially secure independent label: ZTT. Like Stiff, ZTT had enjoyed a rapid ascent to "major player status" in the early Eighties, mainly due to the unparalleled success of their first signing, Frankie Goes To Hollywood. With hits such as 'Relax' and 1984's summer fire-storm 'Two Tribes', Frankie . . . had become one of the UK's biggest groups, subsequently allowing the label to considerably expand their artistic inventory. By 1985, ZTT had signed acts as diverse as Propaganda, Nasty Rox Inc. and the sublime Grace Jones, all of whom enjoyed a moment or two in the spotlight. Though Frankie's . . . appeal had dimmed by the time of Stiff's absorption into ZTT (ex-lead singer Holly Johnson was busy suing his former employers for unpaid royalties in October, 1987), the company was still sufficiently cash-rich to offer a lifeline to their former competition. ZTT boss Jill Sinclair was optimistic over the new alliance: "I want to expand my companies in many different ways," she said, "Stiff will be a part of that – a very small, but very active part. I want all the creditors to know that Stiff is an ongoing concern." Unfortunately, Stiff boss Dave Robinson wasn't part of ZTT's future. Soon after concluding negotiations with Sinclair, he resigned from "all duties" connected to the label he and Jake Riveria set up some ten years before. Jill Sinclair stated Robinson's decision to move on was "by mutual agreement".

As far as The Pogues were concerned, Stiff's demise set the band free to pursue fresher fields. During the autumn of 1987, the rumour mill sprung into operation, with unconfirmed reports that MacGowan et al. were close to signing an extremely lucrative deal with industry giants, EMI Records. However, The Pogues quickly denied any association with the label, preferring instead to keep the press guessing about their new recorded home. In due course, it was finally announced that the group would operate under their old 'Pogue Mahone' imprint, with distribution for all future releases, eventually going to WEA Records. A new single, quizzically entitled 'Fairytale Of New York', was to mark the beginning of this "new arrangement". When asked what the song was about, Spider Stacy grinned: "It's about getting a Christmas number 1, mate . . ."

'Fairytale Of New York' began life as "a little banjo riff" Jem Finer had been playing around with for some time. "(I) had the idea for 'Fairytale . . .', but the tune was poxy," Finer confirmed to *NME* in December, 1987. "I gave it to Shane, he gave it the Broadway melody, and there it was . . ." The 'Broadway melody' in question was a winsome combination of lilting piano and accordion, that over time and several changes of rhythmic pace, built up to a immensely satisfying orchestral climax, full of plunging violins and upturned cellos. "A bloody awesome musical achievement", as one critic put it, the melodic sensibilities of 'Fairytale . . .' were nonetheless surpassed by the lyrics MacGowan brought to the tune. Another spin on street-life, though this time set in the gutters of Manhattan rather than Kings Cross, Shane's latest tale involved two down at heel lovers, content on the face of it to spend their Christmas trading drunken insults. "Happy Christmas your arse, I pray God it's our last . . ." But behind the apparent facade of mutual enmity, there was little doubt this couple from hell were devoted to each other, their relationship sealed by the disappointments and shattered dreams both had faced since arriving in New York from the old country: "Can't make it all alone, I've built my dreams around you . . ."

To make 'Fairytale Of New York' truly work then, it had to be recorded as a duet. Still, finding a female match for MacGowan's rare vocal blend of "piss and vinegar" was no easy task. When the song first surfaced, it was hoped that bassist Cait O'Riordan might step up to the microphone, but her exit from the band into the arms of Elvis Costello soon put paid to that idea. Salvation eventually came via The Pogues' latest producer, Steve Lillywhite. A veteran of several U2 albums (*Boy*, *October* and *War*) as well as a collaborator with the likes of The

Rolling Stones (1985's underrated *Dirty Work*), Lillywhite was one of a new breed of young, yet seasoned studio technicians who could transform a band's innate musical gifts into concrete sales. He was also married to one of the UK's best singers: Kirsty MacColl.

With benefit of hindsight, MacColl's involvement with The Pogues seemed almost predestined. Her father was none other than Ewan MacColl, the distinguished folk musician/ actor/playwright, whose achievements included the formation of The Critics Group (a body dedicated to the analysis of traditional folk stylings), as well as the co-creation of the BBC's famous 'Radio Ballads' series of the late Fifties/early Sixties. A format comprising original song, instrumental music, sound effects and the recorded voices of "ordinary working men", MacColl's radio ballads were aural tapestries weaving together real stories of fishermen, railroad workers and coal miners with the native noises and music of their community. According to folk expert Laurence Aston, "The radio ballads (led) you effortlessly from song to music to sound to the spoken word and back again – revealing the effect of a way of life upon those who led it . . ." Aside from his involvement with this novel format, Ewan MacColl was also an accomplished songwriter, penning such tunes as 1957's 'The First Time Ever I Saw Your Face' (later made famous by soul singer Roberta Flack), 'Freeborn Man', 'The Manchester Rambler's Song' and a strange little ditty entitled 'Dirty Old Town' – last covered by The Pogues.

Her father's contribution to British folk was inconsequential to the role he played in Kirsty's life. Following Ewan's separation from her mother, Jean Newlove, in the early Seventies, the young Kirsty and her brother Hamish saw their famous dad only at weekends. Yet, as she grew older, MacColl Jr. began to understand the level of admiration he commanded outside the household. "It's misleading to say that I had no contact with (my dad) or I didn't love him," she told *Mojo*'s

101

Rob Steen. "I knew he was great, but when you're told someone's great all the time, I just (thought), well, fine . . . where's me David Bowie records?" When it came time for MacColl to chance her arm in the family business then, a career in folk music was definitely not on the agenda. Indeed, her greatest love turned out to be the music of The Beach Boys.

Instead, she turned to pop, releasing her first single, the Motown-inflected 'They Don't Know', in 1979 at the tender age of 19. Though 'They Don't Know' initially failed to chart (the song subsequently became a big hit for comedienne Tracey Ullman), Kirsty's second stab at stardom was far more successful. 'There's A Guy Works Down The Chip Shop, Swears He's Elvis', released by Polydor Records in June, 1981, was a humorous, if occasionally terse, little tune that showcased MacColl's bell-like vocals to sonorous effect. Reaching number 19 in the UK, 'There's A Guy . . .' set the vocalist up for a sustained run of future hits, including an inspired cover of Billy Bragg's 'A New England' and the beautiful 'Days', as well as studio collaborations with the likes of The Rolling Stones, The Smiths, The Talking Heads and Led Zeppelin's Robert Plant. A much in demand session singer and performer in her own right, The Pogue's acquisition of Kirsty MacColl was a positive boon, ably ensuring that 'Fairytale Of New York' would have just the right blend of vocal spit and polish.

When Kirsty first heard the song, she was struck by its obvious chart potential: "To tell, the truth," she later told *Q,* "I was never that bothered by folk music. I was really into The Beach Boys . . . (but) when I first heard 'Fairytale . . .', I really wished I'd written it. It was a classic . . . but Shane's an incredible songwriter, timeless songs – poetic, melodic, whatever . . ." In stark contrast to what was usually required of her, MacGowan asked MacColl to keep her singing as forthright as possible, with little or no vocal gymnastics.

"It was a bit different to the stuff I normally do," she later admitted. "(That's) usually very lush, with lots of harmonies. 'Fairytale' was really straightforward, and I actually found that a bit of a challenge . . . but I really enjoyed doing it." The eventual result of Kirsty's studio duet with Shane was nothing short of inspired, their vocal trades invoking a sense of anger and tenderness with which many a rowing couple could easily identify: "I coulda been someone," howled MacGowan in protest. "Well, so could anyone . . ." came MacColl's icy riposte. " 'Fairytale . . .' is true to life," Jem Finer cheerily confirmed. "More people argue, get divorced and commit suicide at Christmas than at any time of the year . . ."

Released on November 28, 1987, 'Fairytale Of New York' catapulted into the UK charts at number two, the song's immediate success making it an obvious "shoo-in" for the coveted Christmas number one slot. To aid sales, The Pogues appeared with Kirsty MacColl on *Top Of The Pops*, though for some, the thought of starring on Great Britian's highest rated music programme far outweighed the actuality of the event itself. "I used to watch my favourite groups on *Top Of The Pops* when I was a kid," bassist Daryll Hunt later said. "(But) once you're there, it's all a pile of shite. A lot of people getting kicked around by BBC staff. It's not quite as glamorous as you'd think."

Perhaps Hunt drew more satisfaction from filming the promotional video to accompany 'Fairytale . . .', a rambunctious representation of the song's lyrics featuring MacGowan and MacColl battling their way across the Big Apple, while The Pogues looked on from the confines of a smokey bar/studio. Directed by Peter Dougherty (who would forge a long-time filmic association with the band), the 'Fairytale . . .' video also benefited from a 'blink or you'll miss him' cameo from New York actor Matt 'Rumble Fish' Dillon, playing a young policeman who throws Shane in the drunk tank at the start of the tune.

Sadly, no amount of Hollywood-approved cameos or high

profile appearances on British TV could ensure 'Fairytale of New York' went to number one at Christmas. In fact, the song was kept off the UK top spot by The Pet Shop Boys' synthetic interpretation of Willie Nelson's 'You Were Always On My Mind'. MacGowan was quite rightly dumbfounded by the British public's temporary lapse of reason. "The Pet Shop Boys slaughtered 'You Were Always On My Mind'," he later protested. "That's a great Willie Nelson song, a classic version by Elvis Presley, and they took the piss – out of the song, out of the writers, out of the people who bought it."

Spider Stacy was more philosophical in his conclusions regarding 'Fairytale . . .'s stall at number two. "(The song) was a deliberate attempt to get a Christmas number one, and we very nearly pulled it off," he told *Sounds.* "There's nothing wrong with that, but some people might accuse us of being capitalists. But what's the point of living in a fucking garret? It's not about being guilty . . . (it's about) keeping your perspective, remembering what you do is essentially trivial."

In the end, time proved to be on The Pogues and Kirsty MacColl's side. While The Pet Shop Boys version of 'You Were Always On My Mind' quickly faded from public memory, 'Fairytale Of New York' has subsequently enjoyed a rich shelf life, its combination of vicious emotional honesty and surprising musical tenderness as vital today as when it was first released. Joining other seasonal hits such as Slade's 'Merry Xmas Everybody' and Wizzard's 'I Wish It Could Be Christmas Everyday', 'Fairytale . . .' continues to blast from the speakers in pubs, clubs and office parties at a certain time every year: everyone knows the words and sings along – audibly or otherwise. One of those rare gems that tugs at the heartstrings, activates the tearducts and ends all too suddenly, leaving the listener wanting more, 'Fairytale Of New York' forever burned the image of Shane MacGowan into the collective consciousness of UK record buyers – "the Tipperary troubadour" still returning to collect his royalties on an annual basis. With typical alacrity, MacGowan continues to downplay his achievement to this day, perhaps aware that 'Fairytale . . .' now belongs as much to the public as it does to him. Yet, his description of the song remains, much like its writer, the definite article: "It's a sad song . . . a realistic song. That's the only way I could write it, because that's the way it is."

TEN

Cracks In The Armour

If the failure of 'Fairytale Of New York' to hit the top of the singles charts bruised The Pogues' collective ego, they could at least take solace from the resounding commercial success of their third album, *If I Should Fall From Grace With God*, which was finally released on January 30, 1988. Sneaking into the UK Top 30 at number three, the LP doggedly remained a chart fixture for a further sixteen weeks, making it The Pogues' best seller to date. Such a victory was well deserved, as *If I Should Fall From Grace With God* was chockfull of memorable tunes – some of which were rare, yet essential additions to the band's long- established canon of Celtic Folk – while others flirted with far more exotic forms such as rock, jazz and the native music of the Middle-East. In truth, The Pogues' latest offering represented a judicious balance between old and new, allowing them to explore fresh fields without losing sight of the proverbial homestead.

Tellingly, it was also the last time they would manage such a feat without testing the patience of both their core audience and the critics. Still, for the time being at least, the group could bask in the glow of a job well done.

If I Should Fall From Grace With God kicked off in typically violent fashion with the title track, a clattering MacGowan original, rife with images of earthly escape: "Bury me at sea," he growled, "Where no murdered ghost can haunt me . . ." In the time-honoured tradition of 'Down In The Ground Where The Dead Men Go' and 'The Sick Bed Of Cúchulainn', Shane's latest protagonist seemed less interested in divine redemption than the simple pleasures of eternal rest: "Let me go down in the mud where the rivers all run dry." Inspired by MacGowan's visit to the Andalucion desert, where locals fought a long and protracted war to keep the area from the hands of foreign usurpers, 'If I . . .' was actually rejected for inclusion on the soundtrack of Alex Cox's *Straight To Hell*. Yet, Shane persevered with the song until his fellow band members accepted its merits: "It came to me like *that*," he later said. "It was automatic writing – like 'Rainy Night In Soho' . . . just there in five minutes."

Awash with speed-metal banjos and hyper-ventilating penny-whistles, 'If I . . .' might have proved a hard act to follow, but 'Turkish Song Of The Damned' was equal, if not superior to its distinguished predecessor. As much 'desert sand and shale' as 'shamrock and heather', the tune drew its influences directly from indigenous Arabic music, using James Fearnley's inspired accordion playing to emulate Egyptian instruments such as the oud, nay, duf and bendir. Again written by Shane (alongside Jem Finer), 'Turkish Song Of The Damned' returned to the grave for inspiration, though this time, the dead were rising from their tombs to exact a terrible revenge upon the living: "I come old friend from hell tonight . . . to claim a debt from thee." Bizarrely, MacGowan found the title to his tale of other-worldly vengeance through mishearing a question posed by a German fan: "Have you heard 'The Turkish Song' by The Damned?" The rest, as they say, is history . . .

'Bottle Of Smoke', which followed, was another magnificent creation from the play-pen of MacGowan and Finer, its frenetic pace perfectly complimenting the story of a serial gambler finally cracking the big bet: "Like a streak of light, like a drunken fuck, up came the Bottle of Smoke." As the titular horse finally sails past the winning post, beating all comers (as well as a steward's enquiry), Shane let fly with his one of his best lines yet: "The money still gleams in my hand like a light . . ." "'Bottle Of Smoke' is a great celebration," guitarist Phil Chevron later confirmed. "Not of the underdog, but of the horse with three legs!" Following on from 'Bottle Of Smoke' came 'Fairytale Of New York', its gentle pace something of a blessing after The Pogues' opening salvo, yet the band were back on the move again soon afterwards with Jem Finer's rousing instrumental 'Metropolis'. Doffing its cap in the direction of musicals such as *West Side Story* and George Gershwin's 'Rhapsody In Blue', 'Metropolis' was a witty melding of urban jazz and Irish folk stylings, its leaping penny whistles and subterranean brass stabs recalling the madness of a city during rush hour. The tune also revealed how adept Finer and his companions had become as musicians, with years of almost constant touring sharpening individual skills to an enviable degree.

Phil Chevron's 'Thousands Are Sailing' was up next. More contemporary adult rock than traditional ceilidh music, the song nonetheless offered compelling evidence that Shane MacGowan wasn't the only gifted lyricist in The Pogues' ranks. A time-spanning tale that commemorated the men and women who died trying to escape poverty and famine on the "Coffin ships" sailing from Eire to America during the mid-19th century, 'Thousands . . .' also cast a cynical eye on the fortunes of current Irish immigrants making a new life for themselves in The States: "Postcards we're mailing of sky-blue skies and oceans . . . from rooms the daylight never sees, where lights don't glow on Christmas trees . . ." Destined to become a in-concert highlight, the black-eyed charms of 'Thousands Are Sailing' had particularly impressed *If I Should Fall From Grace With God*'s producer, Steve Lillywhite: "I'm especially pleased for Philip that 'Thousands . . .' has become a crowd favourite," Lillywhite later stated. "The Pogues make (that) song live on stage now . . ."

Lighter in tone, though no less effective for it, was 'Fiesta'. One part Benny Hill theme tune, one part *Carry On Abroad* and one part genuine love letter to Spain, 'Fiesta' was The Pogues at their most irreverent, pouring musical sangria all over MacGowan and Finer's ode to Mediterranean excess: "We have the song of the chochana, we have brandy and half corona." Destined for moderate chart success ('Fiesta' reached number 24 in July, 1988), the song's video was notable if only for the fact that it was directed by Ade Edmundson – otherwise known as 'Vivian the homicidal punk' from the BBC's timeless comedy *The Young Ones*.

Reticent to let their 'love of the classics' slide into disrepair, The Pogues next offered up a medley of traditional Irish tunes, including 'The Recruiting Sergeant', 'The Rocky Road To Dublin' and that hoary old standard 'The Galway Races'. In the case of 'The Recruiting Sergeant', humour was back on the agenda as a military man (voiced by MacGowan) tries in vain to persuade a young buck (voiced by Terry Woods) to join him in the trenches: "The king, he is in need of men . . . a life in Flanders for you then would be a fine vacation now." "That maybe so," the lad replied, "but tell me Sergeant Dearie-oh . . . if I had a pack stuck on my back, would I look fine and cheerie oh?" As the lyric progressed towards its conclusion, the listener became increasingly aware that if any fighting was to be done by this particular youth, it was to be under the flag of Republicanism: "I'm not going to Flanders no, there's fighting in Dublin to be done, let your sergeants and your commanders go . . . let Englishmen fight English wars."

If 'The Recruiting Sergeant' hinted at turbulent events in Ireland's past, then 'Streets Of Sorrow' and 'Birmingham Six' concerned themselves with much more recent troubles. In the case of 'Streets Of Sorrow', Terry Woods had written a stark, questioning ballad that brought into sharp focus the thousands of lives lost to sectarian violence in Belfast and beyond: "I'll not return to feel more sorrow, nor to see more young men slain." As Woods' voice faded into oblivion, a powerfully struck acoustic guitar announced the arrival of Shane MacGowan's most daring song yet – the hellacious 'Birmingham Six'. Recounting the events that led to the incarceration of ten Irishmen (including The Guildford Four) for a spate of bombings on the English mainland in the early Seventies, Shane's contention was that these men were innocent of the murders for which they were convicted: "They were picked up and tortured, and framed by the law . . . the filth got promotion, but they're still doing time . . ." In fact, at the time of 'Birmingham Six's release, each prisoner had already spent over a decade behind bars.

While many agreed with MacGowan's version of events – including several prominent defence lawyers, who were in court fighting an appeal on the men's behalf – the sentiments he expressed in 'Birmingham Six' were still extremely contentious. After all, pouring scorn on the British legal system was one thing, but openly stating that ten Irishmen had been falsely imprisoned through the complicity of police and judges was quite another. Shane remained diplomatic when questioned over his lyrical stand. Yet, he did not back down: "It's not a song I enjoyed writing, or find much pleasure in singing," MacGowan later confirmed, "(but) it's a situation that's still going on, which is obscene." His fellow band members were unequivocal in their support – both of Shane's right to voice his opinion, and the opinion itself: " 'Birmingham Six' dares to say that people who are convicted for terrorist bombings might be innocent," Spider Stacy told *Melody Maker*. "It implies that Irish people might be disadvantaged when it comes to British justice." Phil Chevron took the argument one stage further: "If 'Streets Of Sorrow' or 'Birmingham Six' has any effect on these people getting free, then it'll be worthwhile. The songs just states the truth as far as I'm concerned."

Somewhat inevitably, MacGowan's tuneful tirade against

"the whores of the Empire" soon garnered the attention of the British Government, who responded in kind by slapping an immediate radio ban on both 'Streets Of Sorrow' and 'Birmingham Six'. For Shane, such a response was nothing short of political overkill: "We didn't threaten *anybody*," he protested. "All we did was write a song about what's happening."

Again, it was left to Spider Stacy to take the philosophical high ground: "If (the government) had kept quiet about 'Streets Of Sorrow/Birmingham Six', the song would have faded into the mists of time like all the other songs on *If I Should Fall From Grace With God*. Now, they've made it more than just a song. (But) it was (always) more than a song about injustice to Irish people. It's (about) a situation that occurs in virtually every country in the world." Ultimately, MacGowan would be proved right in his assertions regarding the vagaries of British justice. By April 1991, both the Birmingham Six and Guildford Four had their original convictions quashed by the courts, walking away as free men after nearly two decades of wrongful constraint. The government's ban on public airings of 'Streets . . . /Birmingham . . .' was lifted soon after.

If I Should Fall From Grace With God's concluding tracks were considerably less radical than those that immediately proceeded them. 'Lullaby Of London' for instance, was an uplifting, occasionally poignant tale of a drunken father singing his son to sleep. Featuring MacGowan's best vocal performance on the LP, the song's message seemed simple enough: "I'll make sure all's well in your world, if not in mine." 'Sit Down By The Fire', on the other hand, heralded a welcome return to the musical values presented on *Red Roses For Me*, all crashing drums, howling pipes and machine-gun patter: ". . . Lie near the wall . . . cover your head, good night and God bless . . . now fuck off to bed." "(Sit Down By The Fire) is about the old ghost stories people used to tell you in Ireland before you went to bed," Shane later told journalist Gavin Martin, "horrific stories that prepare you for the horrors of the world ahead . . ."

'The Broad Majestic Shannon' was a gentler proposition altogether, with MacGowan waxing lyrical about the passage of time, and the effect it has on small Irish communities: ". . . The next time I see you we'll be down by the Greeks . . . whiskey on Sunday and tears on our cheeks." A beautiful ballad that metaphorically traced Ireland's longest river from its origins in County Cavan to its exit into the Atlantic Ocean via Limerick, 'The Broad Majestic Shannon's sanguine melody bore more than a passing resemblance to 'Fairytale Of New York' – a fact not lost on its writer, who later inferred that Jem Finer had swiped '. . . Shannon's principle riff and stuck it into 'Fairytale . . .', thus earning himself a co-writing credit on the song – and 50% of the royalties every time "the bells rung out for Christmas day . . ." Charges of wilful appropriation, downright theft or sheer bloody coincidence aside, *If I . . .*'s final moment came in the form of 'Worms', one minute and three seconds of musical insanity provided by Andrew Ranken and James Fearnley. A traditional tune (and the term is used loosely), 'Worms' combination of creaking accordions and dissonant cello marked the cod-vocal début of Ranken, whose Bernard Bresslow-like intonations forced one critic to conclude that "The Clobberer sounds like a cross between Tom Waits and Ivor Cutler . . ."

Released in the same year as Morrisey's sterling *Viva Hate*, Crowded House's *Temple Of Low Men* and Van Morrison and The Chieftains' *Irish Heartbeat*, *If I Should Fall From Grace With God* brought The Pogues within spitting distance of real superstar status, the LP's cross-pollination of rock, world music and folk stylings providing the band with enough rope to swing across the chasm from cult respectability to enduring mainstream acceptance. That Steve Lillywhite had played a part in this move towards commercial accreditation was beyond doubt – his influence writ large on tracks such as 'The Turkish

Song Of The Damned', 'Thousands Are Sailing' and 'Birmingham Six' – all epics in their own right, all benefiting from the
producer's deft touch. "Steve's one of the nicest people I have
ever met," MacGowan later confirmed to *Q*, "and he has the
softest, gentlest eyes you've ever seen." Lillywhite was equally
complimentary of his latest charges, revelling in the fact that
they had brought completed songs to the studio rather than
the fragmented chord structures groups such as U2 initially
worked from. Yet, it was worth remembering that The Pogues
had been playing many of the tunes featured on *If I . . .* in
concert for over a year, fine-tuning melodies, dynamics and
rhythmic shifts under the expectant gaze of their ever-growing
audience.

For the critics, *If I Should Fall From Grace With God* was also an
unqualified success, the album marking The Pogues' gradua-
tion from folk terrorists to artistic renaissance men, capable of
turning their hand to almost any musical genre: "The band is
on superlative form during sustained bouts of cultural ransacking that extend from as far afield as the Mediterranean for
'Turkish Song Of The Damned' and beyond for 'Fiesta', with
its bizarre makeshift carnival sound complete with Tijuana
brass and zydeco accordion," reasoned *Q*'s David Sinclair. "As
for MacGowan, his bronchial brogue draws out the thread of
poignant melancholia that is rapidly becoming the group's
strongest card. Not content, then, with upsetting the folk
applecart, The Pogues proceed to erect an exotic fruit stall of
their own." *Sounds*' Neil Perry was equally giving in his assessment of The Pogues latest brush with greatness: "Within the
grooves of *If I Should Fall From Grace With God* you get heaven
and hell and everything in between," stated Perry. "Whether
Shane MacGowan intended the road to run this far when he
first lurched from his surrogate Kings Cross home to sing with
the yobbish Nipple Erectors is irrelevant. What is important is
he has risen to become a vocalist of sparkling clarity. He
weaves stories of instant emotion and saturnine simplicity that

treat life and death with equal amounts of respectful abandon. The sound of a man, and a band, in full bloom."

With their recorded reputation now re-established, The Pogues set off on a comprehensive world tour to promote *If I Should Fall From Grace With God*. First stop was Australia, whose citizens were busy celebrating their country's bi-centenary when the band arrived. In a show of solidarity with Oz's original tenants, The Pogues took to foisting the Aborigine flag above the stage at gigs. Unfortunately, nobody told the group they were actually flying the pennant the wrong way up until several shows into the tour: "Fuck," being Spider's measured response at the time. The Pogues fared far better on UK soil, where they returned in the early spring of 1988 for a string of concert dates. Kicking off at Birmingham's cavernous NEC on February 24, the band appeared at Newcastle City Hall (26), Leeds University (March 1) and Leicester's De Montford Hall (11), before making an impressive six-night stand at London's Town And Country Club in mid-March.

The obvious highlight of their "T&C residency" was an anarchic set performed on St. Patrick's Day (March 17), which The Pogues filmed and subsequently released as a long-play video. Guests on the night included Joe Strummer, who joined the band on-stage for spirited re-working of 'London's Calling', ex-Special Lynval Golding who appeared on 'Rudy, A Message To You' and Kirsty MacColl, who both outsang Shane and outdanced Spider on 'Fairytale Of New York', 'Lullaby Of London' and 'Turkish Song Of The Damned'. For MacColl, appearing live was still a fairly novel experience, the singer having suffered from stage-fright throughout much of her career: "I couldn't breathe," she said of her condition. "I'd be so tense and pent up, I couldn't inhale properly . . . it made me think why does anyone do this? It took me a long time to get over it – but it's like anything else, you just have to really want to overcome it. I just felt that I'd spent years and years in the studio . . . sung in front of all these great musicians and (wasn't) embarrassed by that, so why should I be embarrassed when a few hundred people who aren't musicians come in to watch?"

The Pogues' set list for the *If I Should Fall From Grace With God* tour was a pleasing mixture of old and new. For every established crowd favourite such as 'The Sick Bed Of Cúchulainn' or 'Streams Of Whiskey', there was also an unexpected blast from the past, with 'Kitty' and 'Greenland Whale Fisheries' both being taken out of mothballs for an in-concert spin. The band also previewed much new material, including the chaotic 'Boat Train', 'Bottle Of Smoke' and the infamous 'NW3'. Two tunes that greatly benefited from their transfer from studio to stage were Shane's understated '. . . Rainy Night In Soho' and the instrumental medley 'Battle March' – a musical showcase for Terry Woods, Jem Finer and James Fearnley. Of course, one of the great Pogues songs – 'If I Should Fall From Grace With God' – was also omnipresent, its breakneck pace allowing audiences an opportunity to drop their pints and pile onto the dancefloor. However, 'If I . . .' performed disappointingly when released as a single in March, 1988, only reaching number 58 in the charts.

By that time though, The Pogues had bigger fish to fry. Since being released in the USA, the group's third LP had garnered excellent reviews and was beginning to generate serious chart action, débuting at number 88 on *Billboard*'s Hot 100 and selling 200,000 copies in the process. Knowing that they had to take advantage of this change in their Stateside fortunes, The Pogues spent the next five months touring every nook and cranny of North America. One particular concert of note occurred in New Orleans' Tiptina's club – once a semi- permanent home to the legendary blues pianist Professor Longhair: "We really had to play down there," Phil Chevron confirmed, "I mean *really* play. There's just so much good music about that these crowds want to judge you accordingly. It's both exciting and humbling as the audience

115

are so discriminating, and you're surrounded by a wealth and a tradition of brilliant American music." In addition to the Tiptina's date, The Pogues also appeared at Tommy's in Dallas as well as San Francisco's prestigious Filmore Auditorium, where acts such as The Grateful Dead, Janis Joplin, Jefferson Airplane and John Cipollina's underrated Quicksilver Messenger Service created their live reputations some two decades before.

When it was announced that The Pogues had secured the support slot on Bob Dylan's latest US tour (in promotion of the LP *Down In The Groove*), cracking the States seemed almost perfunctory. After all, here was another ready-made audience appreciative of both traditional sounding music and clever wordplay. If The Pogues could secure their grace and favour, the battle for America was surely complete. Sadly for Mac-Gowan, it was all a step too far. While checking in at Heathrow Airport to fly out to the States, Shane collapsed in a heap. Obviously too ill to travel, The Pogues completed ten dates on the Dylan tour without him: "Other groups in a situation like that would've either said 'Let's get rid of the guy', or 'Let's split up', but we're not the sort to do that. We're all part of each other's problems – whether we like it or not." MacGowan saw his temporary brush with liver disease somewhat differently: "I didn't do the Dylan shows because I was too ill with hepatitis to perform," he later told *Vox*. "I was physically unable to perform. I like to play, I like to write, but I'm not a performing donkey, right?"

In truth, MacGowan's physical collapse was symptomatic of The Pogues' overall state of health in 1988. After nearly five years of live performances, various recording commitments and seemingly endless drinking bouts, the band were beginning to crack under the strain. Andrew Ranken, for instance, had contracted blood poisoning in his hand, due to a recurring injury brought about by his unusual drum technique. Jem Finer was also a casualty of the 'rock'n'roll wars', having suffered several bouts of influenza in rapid succession. On the advice of his wife's Chinese herbalist, Finer gave up all red meat, dairy produce and, most tellingly, alcohol in an effort to stabilise his immune system: "I thought, fuck it . . . I'll give it a try." In the case of Spider Stacy, an Olympic level predilection for cigarettes and alcohol, coupled with a vampiric aversion to the sun had played havoc with his communication skills: "I feel like death," Stacy told *NME*'s Sean O'Hagan at the time. "Like I've been lying on a slab for weeks. It's punishing, fatigue . . . shit. I can't even speak proper English anymore. (I) just don't seem to have the time to relax, to recover . . ." Sadly, Stacy's marriage to his American wife would soon crumble under the strain of simply being a Pogue: "Boozing wrecked my marriage," he later confirmed. "I don't blame her for not putting up with my drinking . . . so (the separation) was perfectly amicable."

Ultimately, Shane MacGowan shouldered the lion's share of ailments within The Pogues' ranks, his casual attitude to bodily upkeep leading to several visits to the doctor. Aside from hepatitis, MacGowan also contracted an earlier bout of pneumonia while on tour in Sweden, as well as a long-term stomach problem brought about by heavy drinking: "I was doing a lot of whiskey," he told the *Sunday Tribune*. "It started doing my stomach in – I wasn't eating enough. Anyway, it was leading to an ulcer, but I never got the fucker." Stories persist, however, that Shane didn't take the medical warnings he received with any great solemnity, choosing to down his anti-ulcer medication with lashings of brandy. Nonetheless, when confronted with accusations that both he and his fellow band members were the architects of their own physical demise, or at least overdoing it on the late nights and spirits, his response was to point towards his contemporaries: "Listen," he said, "every band drinks. It's what they *do*. We're no fucking different."

Despite the cracks starting to appear in The Pogues'

collective armoury, there would be no immediate end to the maladies/woes they were facing. Due to financial problems at Stiff, the band were unable to put out an LP for nearly three years. Therefore, lacking the comfort zone that song-writing and performance royalties might bring, they had little alternative but to hit the road: "The touring has been more or less continuous for the past couple of years," Andrew Ranken confirmed at the time, "but that's partly necessity. We've so many wages to pay . . . we want to be sufficiently successful to tour when we want to, take time off when we want to . . . (After all), most of us are either married or with children." Yet, The Pogues were in no position to take their foot off the proverbial gas. 'Fairytale Of New York' and *If I should Fall From Grace With God* had proved to be massive sellers, and ticket demand for their shows was at an all time high. To capitalise on their current success, and build foundations for their future, the group had to keep going – whatever the short-term cost.

Unfortunately, mid-Nineties wisdom about exploiting an artist's creative and financial possibilities through taking long breaks between albums, staggering touring schedules and the use of video and TV appearances as key promotional tools were not wholly in effect in the late Eighties. Instead, a band at that time was expected to take on the aspect of a war machine, straddling continent after continent until all territories were effectively conquered. In The Pogues' case, however, they had been waging various campaigns without benefit of rest for almost five years, carrying their injuries from battlefield to battlefield and, more often than not, anaesthetising them with alcohol as and when the situation demanded. Unless they now tempered their enthusiasms, or at least sought refuge from their wilder excesses, short-term concerns might well spiral into long-term problems – causing a potentially deadly wear and tear on their creative impulses as well as putting their future prosperity into doubt. While the majority of the band were pragmatic enough to apply the brakes before disaster struck, Shane MacGowan chose instead to place his foot firmly on the accelerator pedal, with all too predictable results.

ELEVEN

Democracy In Action

Despite their collective woes, The Pogues continued on the campaign trail throughout much of 1988, finally ending the year with a string of Yuletide shows at Glasgow's SECC (December 9), Birmingham's NEC (12), Manchester's Apollo Theatre (14/15), London's Wembley Arena (17) and Brixton Academy (19). Eager not to stray too far from the charts, the band also issued a new single just in time for Christmas. Entitled 'Yeah, Yeah, Yeah, Yeah, Yeah', the song was a far cry from the banshee howls of yore, sounding more like a collision between The Rolling Stones and Diana Ross & The Supremes. Written by MacGowan, 'Yeah . . .' was structurally weak in places, its chorus sounding particularly tired and listless: "The strings aren't high enough," Shane later confirmed, "the bass isn't right . . . but I can't complain as I was out to lunch at the time and couldn't get it together." Daryll Hunt disagreed: "It's probably the sexiest record we've ever made," the bassist said. "It really pumps it out." Backed by a wanton treatment of 'The Limerick Rake' and a truly diabolical version of The Stones' 'Honky Tonk Women', 'Yeah, Yeah, Yeah, Yeah, Yeah' stumbled into the charts at number 43, before rapidly disappearing into the musical ether.

Seemingly incapable of rest, the group plied their wares across Europe for much of early 1989, even finding time to return to the States and Australia for the short 'Slaughtered

120

Lambs Of New Wave' tour. Nonetheless, casualties were beginning to mount up. While supporting reggae giants UB40 at St.
Andrews football ground in June, a "barrier crush" ensued in
front of the stage during The Pogues' set, forcing them to
temporarily abandon festivities until order was restored. With
over 100 hundred fans subsequently injured in the fracas, it
was difficult not to draw analogies with the tragedy which
occurred at Hillsborough Stadium only two months before. In
that incident, ninety-five Liverpool supporters were crushed to
death due to overcrowding on the terraces of Sheffield
Wednesday's home ground: "It was outrageous to put people
in a place like that," MacGowan later said of the St. Andrews
gig. "After seeing what happened at Hillsborough, it seems
even more outrageous to hold a gig at a football stadium. If a
bunch of people got killed at one of our gigs, I wouldn't play
ever again. I'm not interested in causing a single piece of
human suffering just for the sake of a fucking pop concert."

In fact, Shane was becoming rapidly disenchanted with
"fucking pop concerts" in general – especially his own: "I hate
the fucking sight of touring," he growled in the summer of
1989. Yet, escape was impossible. In July, The Pogues again
headed across the Atlantic to perform in front of a nuclear
submarine at Riverstage in New York City. Supported by the
Violent Femmes and Mojo Nixon – an act best known for persuading Hollywood actress Winona Ryder to appear in the
video for their single 'Debbie Gibson Is Pregnant With My
Two-Headed Love Child' – MacGowan and friends turned in a
creditable enough set, with highlights including 'A Pair Of
Brown Eyes', 'Broad Majestic Shannon' and a tearaway version
of 'Transmetropolitan'. But one had to question the motives
behind their appearance. Though the novelty value of coupling
pop music with the might of the American military ensured
maximum publicity value for the group, Shane had often publicly disavowed the use of weapons as a means of ending conflict, choosing instead to repeatedly preach the values of

humanitarianism. Now he found himself singing love songs while standing in the shadow of nuclear weapons. Though MacGowan made no comment at the time, the irony could not have been lost upon him.

Or perhaps he was just too tired to care. Compelling evidence for the latter opinion came in late July, 1989 with the release of The Pogues' fourth LP, *Peace And Love*. A disjointed follow up to the superlative *If I Should Fall From Grace With God*, *Peace And Love* meandered between the great, the good and the downright bloody ordinary, revealing The Pogues to be a band in crisis – steadily buckling under the weight of their own internal contradictions. With only six new MacGowan compositions on show, it was left to Jem Finer, Terry Woods and Phil Chevron to take hold of the song-writing reins, leading to a schizophrenic clash of styles ranging from cod-jazz noodling to effete-sounding power ballads. In fact, The Pogues' trademark mangling of Irish traditional music was conspicuous by its absence, the accordions and banjos now taking second place to the steady hum of electric guitars.

Of course, they were highlights: Shane's 'White City' for instance, throbbed along nicely, its lyric bemoaning the conversion of West London's famous greyhound track into a *BBC* building: "And the hare upon the wire has been burnt upon your pyre . . ." "My old man used to go to there, though I only went a few times," MacGowan later confessed. "He was a serious better – used to go to the races and the dogs a lot." To the Pogues singer, demolishing White City was akin to "knocking down a cathedral . . . worse! People used it, it was a living thing, a remarkable building everybody knew. There was a tube station named after it, a whole *area* named after it, and 'bang!', it's gone . . ." Sadly, the gamblers who once frequented the dog track didn't feel the need to commemorate its passing by buying 'White City' when it was released as a single in August, 1989. In fact, it was the first Pogues record in over four years that failed to chart.

Other peaks on *Peace And Love* included Terry Wood's 'Young Ned Of The Hill', a seething tune that damned English general Oliver Cromwell's forced uprooting of Irish landowners in the 17th century: "A curse upon you Oliver Cromwell," growled Woods, "you who raped our motherland, I hope you're rotting down in hell for the horrors that you sent." Jem Finer also provided one of *Peace And Love*'s finer moments with the touching ballad, 'Misty Morning, Albert Bridge': "Held a match to your cigarette, watched the smoke curl in the mist . . ." A song about Jem's hatred of being away from his wife whilst on tour, 'Misty Morning . . .' also featured a fine hurdy-gurdy solo on an instrument Finer built from scratch in his living room: "It's such a brilliant, beautiful ballad," MacGowan later told *Q*'s Adrian Deevoy. "I couldn't have written that. I just couldn't write something that *open*." When released as a single, 'Misty Morning, Albert Bridge' reached a lowly number 41. In truth, it deserved better.

Of *Peace And Love*'s remaining compositions, only Phil Chevron/Daryll Hunt's 'Blue Heaven' and Shane's 'Down All The Days' and anarchic 'Boat Train' truly held one's attention. In the case of 'Blue Heaven', Chevron and Hunt had constructed a pulsating little tune, full of clever chord trickery and baffling lyrical twists: 'Card sharks and blue harps and dolphins who leap in my blue heaven.' 'Down All The Days', on the other hand, was a typically blunt MacGowan original, regaling the achievements of Irish novelist Christy Brown, a man who despite suffering from cerebral palsy (which left him almost incapable of speech and movement) still managed to write books with the toes of his left foot: "I type with my toes, suck stout through my nose . . ." Originally submitted for the soundtrack of *My Left Foot*, director Jim Sheridan's Oscar-winning movie celebrating the life of Brown, (the song was never used), 'Down All The Days' actually played havoc with the facts of Christy's disability – for instance, he never placed a straw in his nose to drink Guinness. Yet, Shane still managed to capture the spirit of the man in all his tragi-comic glory: "The tap-tap tapping of the typewriter pays."

'Boat Train' was another in a long line of MacGowan songs that combined alcohol, gambling, "a bit of casual pilfering and the odd fight" in the space of just under three minutes. Recounting a particularly eventful train/ferry journey between Dublin and London via Hollyhead, Shane's drunken protagonist manages to lose both his money and possessions, break a shin-bone and wake up "in the toilet" before "staggering up the platform off the boat train." Based on a real-life experience MacGowan had some years before, which ended with a strip search at Liverpool Docks – "(They stuck) a flashlight up my arse" – 'Boat Train' captured in hyper-realistic form all the agony and ecstasy of the pilgrimage many Irish men and women make each year to see their in-laws – to wit, endless hours of crushing boredom, sea-sickness and chilly winds only partially alleviated by the presence of drink and playing cards.

Regrettably, beyond 'Boat Train', 'Misty Morning, Albert Bridge' and the likes of 'White City' and 'Blue Heaven', *Peace And Love* offered little more than dull tunes and obvious re-treads of earlier, far superior material. Jem Finer's 'Night Train To Lorca' was 'Turkish Song Of The Damned' in all but name, while Phil Chevron's sickly sweet duet with Kirsty MacColl, 'Lorelei', must have had many a listener recoiling from their stereo-speakers in abject horror. In short, though there was the odd work of genius to admire, *Peace And Love* sounded for the most part a laboured compromise, the forward momentum of *If I Should Fall From Grace With God* lost to increasing factionalism within the Pogues' ranks. The music press sounded caution: "*Peace And Love* is a painful, often wretched testament to the past seasons of Poguetry," said *NME*'s Stuart Bailie. "Personality disorders, intrigue, creative blocks and physical abuse are all in order here. The Pogues, champions for so long in the fine art of brinkmanship, have gone perilously close to that final, frazzled charge over the edge." Bailie continued: "Shane goes meandering after his own fashion. He's still a compelling artist – one of the best we have – but there's nothing here in the league of 'A Pair Of Brown Eyes', 'The Old Main Drag' or the other masterful things he's done already. And on *Peace* . . . , he's clearly lost the plot."

Q's Mark Cooper was a little more giving of The Pogues' latest effort: "By rights, The Pogues should surely be dead by now, overcome by drink, or the enthusiasm of their fans. Yet, somehow they've survived the endless nights of dancing and debauchery, combining their unflagging commitment to the crack with an ever broadening musical and lyrical vision. Their fourth album rattles along like an express train with barely a pause for breath, and while the mood of the songs might liter-ally be summed up as 'decay and defiance' rather than 'peace and love' . . . The Pogues offer further evidence that there's more to kicking and screaming than the punks that preceded them ever discovered." However, long-time supporter and Pogues analyst Sean O'Hagan remained less than convinced that there was any life left in the group: "(Peace And Love) is a soundtrack from the disintegration zone. Confused, direction-less . . . often lyrically incoherent, it portrays, with few notable exceptions, a band at the end of its tether."

O'Hagan undoubtedly knew when writing his review of *Peace And Love* what an uphill struggle the album had been to com-plete. In poor health due to incessant touring, and overtly concerned with consolidating their Stateside success, The Pogues were desperate to shed their 'drunken paddy' image once and for all – moving en masse towards a more mature position that embraced rock as well as folk audiences. How-ever, their principal songwriter was, by his own admission, increasingly 'off with the fairies', indulging a Herculean LSD-habit that had him taking "between ten to fifty blotters a day." Now openly dismissive of his fellow band members' "stadium rock" aspirations, MacGowan grew ever more obsessed with the acid-house revolution taking place in London's night-clubs, even going as far as submitting a twenty-four minute dance epic – 'You've Got To Connect Yourself' – for inclusion on the new LP. When returning producer Steve Lillywhite and the group deemed the track unusable, Shane saw the writing on the wall: "It was obvious to me that the band thought I was temporarily insane," he later confessed. "They started to use the fact that I was out of my brain . . . to ignore any suggestions I had."

With benefit of hindsight, The Pogues' collective stance was simple enough to understand. Having spent six years establishing themselves as a major force, the band were not going to throw it all away indulging MacGowan's latest pharmaceutical crusade. Aside from wives and children to support, there was also the not inconsiderable matter of a road crew and administrative staff to take care of. Though Stacy, Finer, Ranken and Fearnley were once content to carry their own equipment to gigs, they now employed as many people as an average high street bank. Consolidation, not experimentation, was obviously the order of the day. That said, establishing a clear musical direction without Shane's input was an almost insurmountable task. Jem Finer, Terry Woods and Phil Chevron all had a way with a tune, but they lacked MacGowan's clarity of purpose, or more accurately, his God-given ability to meld high lyrical drama with three simple chords. To reach a workable compromise then, ground had to be given by each Pogue in turn. Sadly, democracy in action seldom makes for interesting listening, and *Peace And Love* was not the exception that proved the rule.

When MacGowan initially met with the press to discuss the LP, he seemed content enough to tow the company line, deflecting all queries about the band's increasingly rockist sound by casually pleading ignorance: "As far as I'm concerned, I can't see any difference at all," he stated in 1989. "Everything else might have changed, but the original spirit hasn't." Nonetheless, in later years, Shane would confirm that the creation of *Peace And Love* was fraught with difficulties: "It's a dark album . . . (made) under a lot of pressure – and I hated it . . ."

For the time being at least, The Pogues' private battles had little impact on their public profile. *Peace And Love* débuted on the UK charts at an impressive number five (despite the added allure of a hit single) and stuck around in the Top 50 for a further eight weeks. In the US, a marginal slip occurred with the album only reaching number 118, some 30 places lower than 1988's *If I Should Fall From Grace With God*. Nevertheless, if the band could steel themselves, put aside their musical differences and hit the road in support of the LP, America might yet succumb to their charms. Sadly, Shane MacGowan's position on such matters was about to move from "tired and bored" to "downright fucking disinterested".

TWELVE

Be Careful What You Wish For

With the release of 1988's *If I Should Fall From Grace With God*, The Pogues had not so much moved the goal posts as dug up the foundations of the pitch, sliding away from their Irish traditional roots in pursuit of a folk/rock/jazz amalgam that might see them in competition with the likes of U2. Aware that their ransacking of Ceilidh music afforded only a limited shelf-life at best, the group had cunningly used the LP to gain a critical distance from their past infatuations and present a new strategy to their fans – one that both embraced the present musical climate as well as allowing for a subtle modification to their chaotic origins. And it had worked: compositions such as 'Turkish Song Of The Damned', 'Thousands Are Sailing' and 'Fiesta' were all modern anthems, brimming with power chords, luxuriant brass arrangements and multi-tracked vocal harmonies. With the acquisition of Terry Woods, Phil Chevron and Daryll Hunt, The Pogues were now free to explore new sonic vistas – re-write, if you will, the rules they initially applied to their sound and image.

Additionally, in Shane MacGowan, the group had a front-man capable of re-shaping Celtic romanticism to his own ends, melding lyric and melody into something quintessentially time-less and complete. The proof of MacGowan's particular genius came with 'Fairytale Of New York', a song so satisfying in its execution that it remains a stalwart of both radio and TV to this day. Yet, as with all fairy tale romances, reality soon began to seep in between the cracks. Seemingly invulnerable to the excesses of drink and drugs at the start of their career, The Pogues circa 1988–89 were beginning to fall prey to their own immoderation, with the numerous battle scars earned on concert stages now stubbornly refusing to heal. By the time they came to record the follow up to their most successful LP, there was a discernible souring in the ranks with squabbles over musical direction and future tactics superseding the gang mentality that proved so much a part of their early charm. When *Peace And Love* was finally released in the summer of 1989, the schism within The Pogues was apparent for all to see, with the band sounding like an uneasy composite of cavernous rock stylings ('Tombstone', 'Cotton Fields') and whimsical sentimentality ('Lorelei'). That the old venom was still there couldn't be doubted – 'Young Ned Of The Hill', 'Boat Train' and Shane's blunt-edged lyric to 'London You're A Lady' all dripped with requisite malice – yet somehow, the very essence of the group had become diluted by the depth of their ambition.

To compound the problem, Shane MacGowan seemed increasingly bored with the band he had assembled in the first place, inveterately growling about touring schedules and recording commitments to any journalist within earshot. Behind the scenes, a rapid acceleration in his drug and alcohol habits also pointed towards some kind of creative meltdown, the evidence being his limited contribution to *Peace And Love*, with only six MacGowan originals appearing on the final track listing. Tired, increasingly marginalised within The Pogues' ranks and intoxicated to such a degree that standard cerebral functions were now a fond childhood memory, Shane was burning candle-bright in many a music paper's 'next dead celebrity' list. Of course, he refused to pander to such charges, markedly pointing out that: "If I had a death wish, I'd be fucking dead, wouldn't I?" However, concern for MacGowan's health remained a palpable thing, especially when The Pogues again took to the road in support of *Peace And Love*.

While their headlining appearance at 1989's Reading Festival (supported by the likes Of New Model Army, The Wedding Present and Billy Bragg) went creditably enough, subsequent dates on the *Peace And Love* tour found Shane frequently disappearing from view, only to return moments later with a half-drenched pint glass. Lyrics were forgotten, cues missed and on more than one occasion, he appeared oblivious to the fact that he was on stage at all. Inevitably, it was left to 'ragged lieutenant' Spider Stacy to fill in the blanks, with the penny-whistle player frequently stepping up to the microphone to assume the role of front man. In a classic case of "words returning to haunt us", Stacy had argued only recently that the drunken revelries that defined The Pogues' earliest incarnation were a thing of the past: "It's ridiculous," he told *Q*'s Adrian Deevoy. "People still see us as a drunken novelty act even after four albums, seven years and God knows how many successful tours ... it displays an enormous lack of intelligence to dismiss us like that."

Spider's remarks were partially borne out by two additions to "Poguelore". The first was *Completely Pogued*, a 55-minute documentary focusing on the inner workings of the band which was shown at the ICA in November, 1989 as part of the London Film Festival. Instead of presenting The Pogues as a troupe of disorganised alcoholics, *Completely Pogued* displayed a surprisingly dedicated side to the group's character, allowing viewers a first-hand opportunity to see how they approached song construction and concert appearances. All parts of their career were suitably covered, from the home-made video of 1983's 'Streams Of Whiskey' to a studio recording of country rocker Steve Earle's 'Johnny Come Lately', as well as rare live footage of their recent American club tour with Joe Strummer. In addition to the above, comprehensive interviews with each band member were conducted, giving *Completely Pogued* a multi-dimensional air. Shane, for his sins, was captured both sober and, indeed, less so: "I mean, everybody drinks, right?" he guffawed into camera, "unless they don't, yeah? I mean you drink or you don't . . . there's no point messing around. And if you drink . . . well, you get drunk, right? I mean that's the point of it, innit? I mean, I'm not drunk and I've been drinking since 10 o'clock this morning . . . (though) I might," he concluded, "be fairly relaxed . . ."

If MacGowan's public pronouncements regarding the demon drink sometimes veered towards a wilful display of 'stating the bloody obvious', his deft touch with a rhyming couplet surely undermined all charges of intellectual laziness. Nowhere was this more apparent than in *Poguetry: The Lyrics Of Shane MacGowan*, a collection of numerous verses – from 1983's 'Dark Streets Of London' onwards – published by Faber & Faber in December, 1989. Joining the plethora of work MacGowan had already unleashed were 29 previously unseen poems as well as numerous illustrations by artist John Hewitt, which sometimes accompanied specific songs, or alternatively, drew out painted images from key phrases or descriptions. For example, a beautifully judged sketch entitled 'Flag Glasgow' presented a Scottish Pogues fan proudly holding aloft a Tri-colour pennant, eyes all the while turned towards the stage in front of him. Acting as a companion piece to Hewitt's artwork were a group of photographs taken by esteemed lensman Steve Pyke, which included Pogues' tour shots and the surreal 'Wall Of Shane' – a poignant montage of the "nine ages of MacGowan", that traced the singer from reasonably fresh-faced insolence in 1987 to the full-on 'psychedelic mountain man' look of 1989. In the book's foreword, Shane found himself described as "A romantic of the urban brutalist school," a statement he found to be "Hilarious . . . a brilliant piece of pretentious prose." A moderate success, *Poguetry* . . . went into its second edition in the summer of 1991.

Back in February, 1990, however, The Pogues played on,

contributing a faithful cover of Elvis Presley's 1957 hit, 'Got A Lot O' Livin' To Do' to *The Last Temptation Of Elvis*, a compilation LP distributed through *New Musical Express* in aid of the Nordiff Robbins Music Therapy Foundation. After that, the group re-teamed with The Dubliners to record 'Jack's Heroes', "Eire's unofficial entry into the World Cup song contest." A paean to the power of Republic of Ireland manager Jack Charlton and his leather-booted charges, the principal refrain of 'Jack's Heroes' was a fairly accurate appraisal of the Republic's even-handed style: "We'll play like gentlemen, to win, to lose, to draw . . ." Yet, the song itself was no '. . . Irish Rover', crawling along on the back of a particularly uninspired melody. 'Jack's Heroes' was also up against some serious chart competition from the likes of Team Scotland's 'Say It With Pride', which attracted vocal contributions from ex-Marillion singer Fish, Runrig and The Silencers and New Order's sterling 'World In Motion' – the official theme tune to back England's World Cup hopes. In the end, 'Jack's Heroes' (written by Spider and Terry Woods) limped into the UK charts at a disappointing number 63, its chances at a higher placing perhaps held back by a frankly appalling video directed by Tim Booth, a man best known for his innovative camera work with The Cure.

In the summer of 1990, however, news arrived that Shane MacGowan was finally ready to call a halt to his recent excesses, having been told by doctors that should he persist with his current level of alcohol abuse, he would be dead "within two years". "If I carry on drinking," he told *Vox*'s Sean O'Hagan, "I'll get cirrhosis of the liver – a slow, agonising death. I've seen people die from it and I don't want anything to do with that. I'm fucked if I'm going to die from drink." MacGowan continued: "I'm 32 years old. With a bit of luck, I'm only half way through my life, right? And I'm fucked if I'm going to waste it doing things people do when they waste their lives . . . achieving nothing in the end." Though Shane had already achieved far more in the last six years than many do in a lifetime remained a moot point. It was still gratifying to hear him speak of the future rather than test the current limits of his endurance. Nonetheless, sobriety seemed to bring about a new set of problems for him – specifically, the musical road The Pogues committed themselves to in 1987: "I think we're wanking out and I don't like it," he gruffly stated. "This stinking business disgusts me. It frustrates me playing 'stadium rock'. To me, stadium rock isn't rock'n'roll . . ."

And there it was in black and white. A sober Shane MacGowan at last admitting to a level of dissatisfaction that had plagued his every move for three long years. Ever the old punk, MacGowan obviously couldn't tolerate the fact that The Pogues were now as much a corporate entity as they were a group of musicians – making compromise after compromise in an effort to sustain their commercial profile. Yet, while his sudden move to the moral high ground was easy enough to champion, Shane could also be accused of intellectual naivety. After all, the rock business was seldom connected with matters of conscience. Like all financial enterprises, it was largely a numbers game, dedicated to shifting records, concert tickets and, increasingly as the Eighties drew to a close, T-shirts. In the end, The Pogues had proved themselves rather good at it, pulling out of the stuffy clubs and pubs that defined their formative existence to ply their trade in theatres, concert halls and, eventually, football grounds. That they made such a transition was in large part due to MacGowan's own songwriting gift and natural flair with an audience. To now accuse his colleagues of "wanking out" sounded somewhat churlish, especially if one considered his early proclamation: "I want to go all the way with this . . ."

Nonetheless, the case for the defence was strong. Once a band dedicated to resurrecting the corpse of Irish traditional music, The Pogues were in real danger of becoming a folk-rock behemoth, their only palpable connection to the bad old days being the behaviour of their wayward front-man. Spider Stacy always said that "The Pogues were about far more than just folk," yet as *Peace And Love* illustrated, when they strayed too far from their roots, their limitations became glaringly apparent. For better or worse, MacGowan seemed to realise this. For him, the very essence of the band was always connected to their irreverence – whether spitting on a poster of Margaret Thatcher in the video for 'A Pair Of Brown Eyes' or regaling British audiences with the word 'arse' on 'Fairytale Of New York' – The Pogues represented a raw blend of punk attitude and outlaw daring. And here they were, hurtling towards the nebulous, often anodyne regions of stadium rock.

As with many a debate, argument or bloody conflict, the truth of the matter was blurred by a combination of past history and current perspective. In a sense, MacGowan was right – both he and The Pogues were a long way from home, their rebel status irrevocably compromised by mainstream chart success and ever-growing ticket demand. Originally perceived as the scourge of the folk establishment, they were now doyens of respectability – admired as much for the authenticity of their earliest recordings as their ability to build upon them. Yet, for Shane to accuse the band of "wanking out" (or, as accurately, 'pursuing the Yankee dollar') was perhaps an insult too far. Having taken the bold step of sublimating their original influences with American, Middle-Eastern and Mediterranean folk stylings, The Pogues had also opened themselves up to a new audience, one far too large to house in the local pub. If they were to sustain this level of interest, then further modifications to their sound and approach were inevitable.

Sadly, all such arguments were rendered obsolete in October, 1990 when The Pogues released their fifth studio album, the portentously titled *Hell's Ditch*. A disastrous confection of anaemic pop tunes, meandering ballads and incomprehensible lyricism, the LP displayed a group at the end of its artistic tether – content to throw crayons at a blackboard rather than place oil on canvas. Of the thirteen tunes presented, Mac-Gowan was responsible, in one way or another, for six in all (sharing co-writing status with Jem Finer on a further three). Therefore, if anyone had to take responsibility for the mess, it was undoubtedly Shane himself: "*Hells Ditch?*" he later grimaced, "(is) an album best forgotten about." Unfortunately he wasn't joking, with only three songs on the record coming away with their dignity intact: In 'Lorca's Novena', at least, MacGowan had constructed a real war anthem, reminiscent of such past glories as 'Boys From The County Hell' and 'Turkish Song Of The Damned': "The years went by and then the killers came," he croaked, "took the men and marched them up the hill of pain." Enlivened by several clever switches in tempo and an emotive Spanish guitar solo from James Fearnley, 'Lorca's Novena' stuck out on *Hell's Ditch* like the proverbial jewel in a dung heap . . .

'Rain Street' too, was moderately entertaining (if a tad forced), with Shane offering up bitter-sweet images of drunken priests, destitute wives and the odd lapse of concentration: "I gave my love a goodnight kiss, I tried to take a goodnight piss . . . but the toilet moved so again I missed." And of course, there was 'Summer In Siam', a composition inspired by the vocalist's extended holiday in Thailand in the summer of 1989: "(It's my) new spiritual home", he offered at the time, "(The song's) saying 'I'm out of my brains, I'm in Thailand and everything is in perfect harmony . . .'" A rolling, good-natured tune featuring emotive turns from Finer and Fearnley on saxophone and piano respectively, 'Summer In Siam' was almost rose-tinted in its lyrical presentation: "The moon is full of rainbows . . ." Elsewhere though, MacGowan's oriental jaunt proved less than inspiring, with the lyrics to 'Sayonara' and 'House Of The Gods' little more than advertisements for whiskey and lager: "Singha beer don't ask no questions, Singha beer don't tell no lies . . ."

Beyond these three songs, *Hells Ditch* floundered. There was the occasional moment of clarity: Spider Stacy's strangely affecting lead vocals on Jem Finer's '. . . Wake Of The Medusa'. The haunting opening bars of the title track. Even MacGowan's surreal, stream of consciousness ramblings on '5 Green Queens And Jean' had their charm. Yet, however one cut the proverbial mustard, *Hell's Ditch* remained a dog of an album. At the time though, critics were curiously reticent to put the knives in: "The sound is coherent," exclaimed *NME*, "the tunes . . . great, the lyrics hilarious. (It's) a great Pogues record. "*The Correspondent* agreed, proclaiming *Hell's Ditch* to be "A fine return to form." Even the *Irish Post* was buoyant in its praise: "Classic stuff from The Pogues." Nonetheless, others cried foul: "*Hell's Ditch* is at best, below par," proclaimed *Melody Maker*'s Andrew Mueller, "at worst, (it's) flat out fucking embarrassing." Fellow *MM* journalist Jon Wilde concurred: "Despite conceding that 'Lorca's Novena' might number amongst MacGowan's finest creations, Shane is not a well man . . . like Dylan and Reed before him, he seemed to work in spite of his vocal limitations . . . he *emoted* rather than sang. On *Peace And Love*, he simply barked. Now, he's reduced to a scabby growl. He sounds bone-tired . . . as though he just can't be bothered. *Hell's Ditch* is not quite a disgrace, but you get the feeling that The Pogues are on the verge of some awful calamity."

As with *Peace And Love*, the making of *Hell's Ditch* was "a nightmare . . . from start to finish". Dispensing with the services of Steve Lillywhite, The Pogues brought in old friend/ occasional band member Joe Strummer to oversee production duties on the album – a decision Shane wholeheartedly backed: "(Joe) created a good vibe . . . a good working atmosphere." Yet, Strummer appeared powerless to halt the schisms that soon appeared within The Pogues' ranks. According to MacGowan at least, both he and Jem Finer found themselves increasingly marginalised in terms of choice of material, with two of their better compositions – 'Pinned Down' and 'Curse Of Love' – rejected in favour of "some real duffers": "The rest of them leave a lot to be desired in the imagination department," he later scowled. Nonetheless, Shane had again fallen off the wagon at the time of *Hell's Ditch*'s recording, a fact made abundantly clear by his vocal performances on the LP. "Without a lyric sheet," reasoned *Sounds*' Leo Finlay, "most of the lyrics (on *Hell's Ditch*) would be rendered incomprehensible, and really, one longs for the days of *Rum, Sodomy And The Lash* . . ." This fact, coupled with MacGowan's domination on the song-writing front, lends little credence to his claim that his fellow band members were largely at fault for the LP's artistic failure.

In the end, apportioning responsibility was, at best, a futile exercise. On the creative ropes for the best part of three years, The Pogues were now a group comprising two discernible factions: Shane and the others. Only Jem Finer seemed able to act as a conduit between each side, sticking up for his friend at every available opportunity: "Yes, he's probably not the healthiest person in the group," said a weary sounding Finer, "but that's *his* business . . ." Entering the UK charts at number 12 (and a lowly number 187 in the US), *Hell's Ditch* spent the best part of five weeks fluttering around the Top 50 before finally giving up the ghost. 'Summer In Siam' – the first single released from the LP – fared even worse, peaking at a miserable number 64 in September, 1990. When a second 45, 'Sayonara', failed to chart, many a critic began writing epitaphs for the group. If The Pogues had chosen to bow out gracefully, or at least take a well deserved break, they might have escaped with their reputation intact – a group fondly remembered as much for their successes as their excesses. Instead, they chose to struggle on, with inevitable consequences.

THIRTEEN

Riding Painted Horses

"You don't form a band to drink milk . . ."
                                    – Shane MacGowan

As The Pogues edged ever closer to their appointment with destiny, a veritable sea change was taking place in British pop. After years of synthesiser-dominated bands, England was once again producing creditable guitar music, mainly emanating from the Manchester region. Acts such as The Charlatans, Happy Mondays and The Stone Roses had infested the charts with a beguiling combination of Sixties psychedelia and dance-inflected grooves, all of which circulated around crisp, no-nonsense guitar riffs. In truth, while the 'Madchester' scene represented no direct threat to MacGowan or his group, the sounds emanating from across the Irish Sea should have given them some cause for concern. In September, 1990, for instance, Dublin chanteuse Sinéad O'Connor walked away from *MTV*'s annual Music Video Awards with three silver trophies – 'Best Video Of The Year', 'Best Female Video' and 'Best Post-Modern Video' – all awarded for her sterling cover of Prince's melancholy ballad 'Nothing Compares 2 U'. Only a month later, Eire's newest folk-rock export, The Hothouse Flowers, began their latest assault on UK audiences, culminating in a sold out appearance at London's Wembley Arena.

Both O'Connor and The Hothouse Flowers were indicative of the changing face of Irish music, reflecting a move towards a new emotional honesty – or "confronting the past with contemporary tools", as one critic would have it. In Sinéad's case, the emphasis was firmly placed on personal catharsis, her lyrical imagery drawn from a seemingly endless well of childhood disturbance, spiritual distress and feminist ideals. With The Hothouse Flowers, it was more about the pursuit of 'peace and harmony', their sturdy brand of romanticism a welcome antidote to Ireland's ever-more business-like image abroad. Though both acts professed an abiding love of The Pogues' music, citing Shane as a particular influence, they also helped define why the band had become increasingly less important in the scheme of things. Once "a vital, swashbuckling alternative to the cold comforts of Irish traditionalism", they were now in real danger of being usurped by the children they helped to spawn. If ever a group needed to come out of their corner fighting, it was surely The Pogues . . .

Regrettably, the band that embarked on a nationwide tour in the autumn of 1990 in support of *Hell's Ditch* more resembled a punch-drunk has-been than an angry young lion – thanks in large part to the lethargic figure at centre-stage. "MacGowan cuts a pathetic, dishevelled figure," stated *Sounds'* Tim Peacock, after witnessing The Pogues at Manchester Apollo, "(looking like) a cross between the PG Tips chimps and a particularly down-at-heel tramp. (He) clings onto the microphone and ever-present bottle for dear life." *Melody Maker*'s Andrew Mueller experienced similar feelings at Glasgow Barrowlands: "Shane started out being heroically wretched," Mueller explained, "graduated to being worryingly broken down and has now reached the stage of pitiful uselessness. The crowd no longer applaud him because they see the hooligan poet of yore spluttering beautiful words about harsh realities – they cheer him because he's a slobbering yob like them. MacGowan," he concluded, "deserves better than this . . ."

As the *Hell's Ditch* dates rolled on, concern for Shane's ever-deteriorating state of health was a major talking point for fans and critics alike. Yet, in a display of impressive loyalty, The Pogues refused to disparage their front man: "(The press) made this myth of Shane as the blundering buffoon more than he has himself," Spider Stacy confirmed. "He's not a complete imbecile who, by some miracle, puts pen to paper . . . and writes beautiful poetry. Shane is very clever. A very gifted individual. Maybe . . . he plays up to this ruffian image . . . but he's no fool." Though such devotion was undoubtedly touching, many felt MacGowan was "on a fast track to oblivion", his increasingly erratic behaviour both on- and off-stage a sure sign of impending doom. Again, any notion of mortality was swept aside, with Jem Finer mounting a particularly spirited defence on his friend's behalf: "Where people make the big mistake (with Shane) is saying he is preoccupied with death," Jem told *NME*. "I don't think he is at all. I think he's obsessed with life . . . what it means to different people in different places at different times."

Finer was correct in his assertions. MacGowan manifested no death wish. Nor was he particularly interested in injuring himself. What he was eager to do, however, was drink, be merry and, if at all possible, avoid damnation – from press, peers and fans. Like thousands of artists before him, Shane could not easily separate alcohol from creativity. In his mind, the two were symbiotically linked: "Drinking stimulates the imagination," he told *Melody Maker*, "the natural ability to rhyme . . . it also stimulates symbolism, which is really important in writing. Reality becomes more acute . . . your subconscious is acting on the same level as your conscious mind. You're using all your senses, as if in a state of meditation, not judging, not asking why, just *experiencing* in its purest form."

In truth, MacGowan's eloquent summation of 'alcohol as a creative tool' was simply a modified coda to previous statements from writers such as Charles Bukowski and Brendan

Behan. Yet, if one added the word 'drugs' to 'drink', then the creative door literally flew off its hinges with a veritable legion of poets, musicians and novelists all queuing up to sanction the truth of Shane's remarks: Coleridge, Shelley, Keats, Byron, Wilde, Yeats, Ibsen, Hemingway, Huxley, Burroughs, Leary, Philip K. Dick, Parker, Davis, Williams, Cash, Morrison, Hendrix, Richards, Lennon, Lynott, Tyler, Kilminster – from peyote-chewing shamen to inner-city speed freaks, the list, as they say, was endless.

Nonetheless, what separated MacGowan from such distinguished company was the sheer ardour with which he attacked his chosen discipline and, more tellingly, the fearless honesty he exhibited when questioned about it. Unlike many of his contemporaries within the music industry, Shane seldom hid his excesses from public view, preferring instead to 'hoist his petard' wherever possible. Of course, he also benefited greatly from the fact that alcohol enjoyed legal status in most countries of the world. If his drug of choice was crack cocaine, then things might have been markedly different. But for the time being at least, The Pogues' singer was free to indulge himself in the full and certain knowledge that he was not breaking the law.

Sadly, MacGowan's quest for 'pure experience' didn't end with a drop of the hard stuff. As previously revealed, he was supplementing an already formidable alcohol habit with liberal helpings of LSD, a chemical renowned for its unpredictable effects on the human brain. This fact, coupled with the warnings he received from doctors regarding cirrhosis of the liver, meant that while Shane's bodily functions were currently firing faster than a Catherine wheel, they were also at risk of permanently burning out. In short, if he wasn't careful, he might just find himself spiralling out of Earth's orbit. "I'm a big boy," MacGowan later confirmed. "I know what I'm doing." Like many around him, Pogues accordionist James Fearnley remained in awe of his front man's proclivities:

141

"I don't know how he does it, I really don't," Fearnley told *Q*. "The annoying thing is he'll probably outlive all of us. In fact, he'll probably do it just to annoy us . . ."

Regardless of MacGowan's growing problems, The Pogues kept up a more or less full schedule throughout the closing months of 1990. After the *Hell's Ditch* tour concluded at Wembley Arena on October 26, they were soon back in the public eye for *Red, Hot And Blue* – a project created "to raise awareness and challenge the stigma surrounding Aids." Joining artists as diverse as U2, The Neville Brothers and one of their own heroes, Tom Waits, the group contributed to a double album "designed to generate funds for victims of the disease." Comprised solely of old Cole Porter songs, *Red, Hot And Blue*'s highlights included Iggy Pop dueting with former Blondie vocalist Deborah Harry on a spirited version of 'Well, Did You Evah', Sinéad O'Connor setting light to 'You Do Something To Me' and Bono and The Edge completely re-inventing Porter's inimitable 'Night And Day'.

In addition to the LP, a TV special – *Red, Hot And Blue, The Film* – was transmitted on ITV on December 1, 1990 (in honour of the newly christened 'World Aids Day'). In essence "a video diary" made to accompany the album, noted independent directors such as Wim Wenders, Jim Jarmusch and Jonathan Demme captured Pop, O'Connor and Waits going through their paces. As far as The Pogues were concerned, they re-teamed with Kirsty MacColl to record one of Cole Porter's better known compositions, 'Miss Otis Regrets/Just One Of Those Things'. Unfortunately, neither the group nor MacColl seemed able to capture the song's ethereal feel, opting instead to re-double its pace and overcrowd it with banjos. To compound the problems, the accompanying video, directed by Neil 'The Company of Wolves' Jordan, was an altogether embarrassing affair, filled with ballroom dancers, Cossack dancers, Irish dancers and, in a link from *The Twilight Zone*, limbo dancers. For his sins, MacGowan appeared thoroughly disinterested by the events none too subtly unfolding around him, and chose, perhaps wisely, to give the limbo stick a miss . . .

Contrary to all good sense, The Pogues were back on the road again by the spring of 1991. That said, the band's two and a half hour set at Glasgow Barrowlands on St. Patrick's Day (17th March) numbered among the best of their career, with 'The Sick Bed Of Cúchulainn', 'Dirty Old Town', 'Thousands Are Sailing' and 'The Irish Rover' all dispatched with both fire and grace. 'Streets Of Sorrow/Birmingham Six' was also particularly poignant, given that the group were joined on stage by Gerry Conlon and Paddy Armstrong – two of 'The Guildford Four' – released after fifteen years of wrongful imprisonment only three days before. For fellow detainee Paul Hill, freedom, however sweet, still couldn't lessen the enormity of the injustice served upon him: "So many people who go into that environment really have no concept of what's happening to them until it's too late," Hill later recalled, "until you're really drowning, you're under the water, gasping for air and you see the light . . . and you're trying to get up and you can't get up. That's exactly what it's like. And no one's going to pull you up – only yourself. A lot of people who go into that environment drown . . . literally drown." The radio ban on 'Streets Of Sorrow/Birmingham Six' was finally lifted in April, 1991.

The following June, a weary looking Pogues headlined Finsbury Park's annual Fleadh Festival. Conspicuous by their absence the year before, Fleadh '91 still presented the group with a reasonable opportunity to gloss over recent failures and re-activate the interest of their home crowd. Yet again The Pogues floundered, handing in a criminally short set rendered almost unlistenable by recurring sound problems. MacGowan, sporting long sideburns, a droopy moustache and jet black leather jacket, spent most of his time drinking from a can of Holsten Pils or firing up a rapidly diminishing supply of Benson & Hedges cigarettes. Suffice it to say, his performance remained undistinguished. For what it was worth, the rest of the day went reasonably well, with support acts Van Morrison, Nanci Griffith and The Saw Doctors all performing lively, if occasionally odd sets.

Despite a glaring need to get off the road, revitalise their energies and write some new songs, The Pogues just kept coming. After appearing on 'Bringing It All Back Home', a five-part TV documentary series looking at the roots of Irish music, the band again found themselves back on-stage at the Brixton Academy on July 15, as part of The Chieftains' music festival – a week long celebration chaired by one of Ireland's best loved instrumental acts. In addition to The Pogues' involvement with these revelries, guests as musically disparate as Marianne Faithfull, ex-Undertone Feargal Sharkey and Kate and Anna McGarrigle all made vocal contributions to The Chieftains' sound at several gigs in the London Area, including the Royal Festival Hall and the Palladium.

With their obligations in Brixton suitably fulfilled, The Pogues next set off in search of 'Feile 1991', a high-profile music event held in Thurles, County Tipperary on August 4. Not too far from Shane's childhood home, 'Feile 1991' went surprisingly well for the group, the crushing sense of tiredness displayed at the Fleadh some six weeks before all but absent from their set.

And then came Japan.

From the off, MacGowan seemed to treat The Pogues' visit to the Land of the Rising Sun as little more than a paid holiday – beginning a week long Saké bender that saw him miss three out of four of the band's scheduled concert appearances. When he did show up, the gig was reduced to a shambles, with Shane more content to sit in a drunken heap by the drum riser than perform his on-stage tasks. For his fellow Pogues, it was all a step too far. Following a hastily arranged group discussion, they confronted MacGowan in his hotel room, making it clear his services were no longer required. Within a week, Spider Stacy broke the news to the press: "(Shane's) simply not interested, and too tired to carry on touring," he told *NME*'s Stuart Bailie. "As far as any further involvement with the band – as far as writing or anything – I honestly don't know. But it seems to me that the time for a clean break . . . if he chooses to . . . has come." When pressed on the subject, Stacy set discretion aside in favour of the plain truth: "You can't be worrying about whether or not somebody's going to be answering a knock in the morning . . . you know what I mean?"

What Spider chose not to reveal was the perilous state of health MacGowan had fallen into by the time of his dismissal. Still seeking medical advice for recurring liver problems, Shane was now also suffering from a debilitating lack of strength in his arms, a condition that would force him to make several visits to a neurologist. In addition to these internal maladies, the singer managed to inflict further injury upon himself by cutting his head wide open while 'on the tiles' in Japan. All in all then, it came as little surprise when MacGowan expressed "relief" on being advised of his colleagues' decision. "If I kept touring," he later conceded, "they'd have to be dragging me out of an old wooden box and sticking an electric current up my arse to get me to perform . . ."

In later years, Shane would often return to the subject of leaving (or being forcibly ejected from) The Pogues, offering a variety of excuses for his unreasonable behaviour: "The whole thing was so shite," he confirmed to the *Irish World*. "I had to lose myself in the drink. I was fed up with the band, the music, the whole thing. I just lost myself." He wasn't exaggerating. Shortly before 'the Japan incident', MacGowan actually admitted himself to a Dublin mental hospital in an effort to stabilise his condition. He was subsequently transferred to a medical centre in Central London where he stayed for a short while before leaving voluntarily. At no time, however, did he consider taking his own life: "The reason I tried to leave The Pogues loads of times, before they were actually kind enough to throw me out, was because I *didn't* have a death wish," Shane stated emphatically. "Life is sweet ..." Truthfully, MacGowan's somewhat ignominious exit from The Pogues was on the cards long before the events of Japan. In fact, he tried – and failed – several times to cut ties with the group, but "responsibility and loyalty" always prevailed: "What, leave the rest of them in the lurch?" Shane told The Fall's Mark E Smith in 1988. "It's a democracy, our band . . ."

With the benefit of hindsight, there is much evidence to support the notion that Shane felt a genuine loyalty to the group he helped form. He took the view that he had to keep working – keep contributing – lest they floundered without his creative input. But rancorous boredom, coupled with a pathological hatred of touring and a profound distrust of the musical direction The Pogues were taking meant that MacGowan was as content to fall upon his sword as have it thrust into him. From his fellow band members' point of view, they had seen their principal songwriter progress from a position of unrivalled strength to relative powerlessness – seemingly more content to ride painted horses on a pharmaceutically assisted merry-go-round than assist them in the process of world domination. In short, Shane had become less an asset, and more a liability. For the sake of his health – and theirs – it was best to let him go.

To the surprise of some critics, The Pogues wasted no time in re-establishing their public profile. Soon after the events of September, 1991, the group announced they would honour all existing tour commitments by supplementing their ranks with old friend/producer Joe Strummer. Brought in to provide lead vocals/rhythm guitar, Strummer talked fondly of the man he was to replace. "The MacGowan songs are really great to sing," he confirmed, "a fine bunch of work to sing." Ever the gentleman, Strummer even posited the notion that Shane might become a Brian Wilson-type figure – staying at home writing songs and even working with the band in the studio while his 'brothers' toured the world on his behalf. Following an uneasy silence from his fellow band members, Joe chose not to mention the idea again.

A live act once more, The Pogues took to the road for the umpteenth time on November 29, 1991, turning in a fine performance at the Cambridge Corn Exchange before venturing across the UK for nine further dates. The tour ended on an exceptionally high note at London's Town & Country Club on December 12, made all the more notable by blistering versions of the old Clash classic 'London's Calling' and the group's adopted anthem 'I Fought The Law'. In fact, it was hard to reconcile this new, musically disciplined fighting force with the ramshackle group that literally fell onto the stage only a year before. Yet, even the harshest critic would agree that something was missing – a spirit, perhaps – but one likely to haunt the family home for some time to come.

To mark this uneasy changing of the guard (or more likely, extract a final commission lest a Shane-less Pogues proved untenable), WEA Records chose to issue a CD retrospective – *The Best Of The Pogues* – just in time for Christmas. An excellent collection, made all the more poignant by the sheer amount of MacGowan compositions on show, *The Best Of The Pogues* pushed the group back into the albums charts, settling in at a comfortable number 12. "Shane MacGowan . . . set himself a truly heroic task," wrote *Q*'s Charles Shaar Murray of the LP. "In the seven year lurch of The Pogues, he . . . distilled an aromatically personal poetic myth from the experiences of 20th-century Irish Diaspora and fused the furious, frantic energies of punk to Irish traditional music. Simultaneously, he has notched the concurrent achievement of accomplishing these feats while seemingly being the most pissed person in the entire universe the whole time . . . Brendan Behan lived to a ripely piratical old age, and here's wishing the same to Shane

147

MacGowan." A re-release of The Pogues' crowning achievement, 'Fairytale Of New York', also dented the charts, reaching number 36 on December 14, 1991.

To underline the relative pathos of the MacGowan/Pogues split, a pre-recorded TV special featuring the band before they parted ways was aired on Christmas Day, 1991. Entitled *The Ghosts Of Oxford Street*, the programme was essentially ex-Sex Pistols manager Malcolm McLaren's homage to the spirit of Dickens, with Malcolm casting himself in the rather choice role of Fagin. A light and fluffy sixty minutes of television, . . . *Ghosts Of Oxford Street* used pop stars and style icons to propel its slim story along, with Tom Jones performing 'Money', Sinéad O'Connor warbling her way through 'Silent Night' and Happy Mondays' Shaun Ryder somewhat implausibly covering The Bee Gees' 'Staying Alive'. The Pogues (including a very hirsute Shane) were cast as McLaren's robber accomplices, though as with *Straight To Hell*, they displayed little in the way of acting skills.

Following the transmission of *Ghosts* . . . all went quiet on The Pogues front. A new single was promised for 1992, but beyond that, the band were reticent to confirm any further plans. MacGowan, too, kept a dignified silence, rarely straying far from his North London home. At least this bout of inactivity allowed fans and critics to ponder the probable futures of both factions. In The Pogues' case, the concern was obvious: having dispensed with Shane's creative input, could they now produce the goods to stay in the spotlight? Assessing MacGowan's chances, however, was a more difficult task. After all, the popularly held belief was that the sheer weight of his excesses had drowned his basic gift, leaving him at best, a spent force. At worst, a physical and emotional wreck. Ultimately, it all boiled down to one emotive question: who would be the victor, and who would be the vanquished?

FOURTEEN

A Period Of Adjustment

Shane MacGowan was sacked from The Pogues in September, 1991. At first, the band made encouraging noises about retaining him in some capacity, whether as in-house songwriter, occasional contributor or honorary mascot, but as the months went by, it became increasingly clear he was no longer a part of their future plans. By taking the bold step of employing Joe Strummer as their new (albeit temporary) frontman for a nationwide tour, The Pogues gained a critical distance from recent failures and re-established themselves as still worthy contenders for the folk-rock crown. Though the Shane-less group were yet to prove themselves in the unforgiving confines of the recording studio, they had at least negotiated 'the first hurdle' with some aplomb. In stark contrast, MacGowan took only three things with him from The Pogues: his name, his talent and his girlfriend. Thankfully, all three could be relied upon in the years to come.

While it would be some time before Shane would again trade on his name and reputation, his devotion to Victoria Clarke remained both constant and touching: "I've got a wonderful girlfriend," he grinned in 1991. Never a man prone to exaggeration, MacGowan was still probably underselling Clarke's contribution to both his physical and emotional upkeep. A striking redhead, she was first drawn into Shane's orbit at the age of 16: "We met in a London pub," Victoria later told the *Daily Telegraph*, "and I didn't like him at all. He was arrogant, stuck-up and not at all attractive. In fact, he was just a bloke who played old Irish songs very badly. But there are certain people you're destined to fall in love with . . . whether you want to or not . . ." Yet, fall in love they did, becoming one of the rock world's more enduring couples. However, MacGowan's love of a drink (or anything else that came to hand) meant her lot was never going to be easy. "I was useful as a kind of nurse/therapist/minder," said Victoria, "who could be relied upon to feel guilty if I didn't manage to get Shane on the tour bus . . . out of the bar or on the stage."

As MacGowan's troubles within The Pogues intensified, Victoria became one of the few cornerstones of his troubled existence. "Touring for three hundred days a year contributed a lot to his mental instability," she later remembered. "Instead of admitting he wanted to leave The Pogues, he'd get really drunk so they'd chuck him out. It was quite literally, driving him mad," she concluded. When Shane finally snapped and entered a hospital for psychiatric treatment, Clarke's solution was to once again don her Florence Nightingale outfit. "In my case, I saw rescuing him from the brink of madness . . . much in the same way other people might view becoming a social worker: as a kind of vocation."

Though Victoria often had to put aside her career as a journalist to tend to MacGowan's needs, regrets were few and far between. "Shane's a very beautiful, lovely kind of person," she confirmed, ". . . sweet, honest . . . he's got a lot of integrity, a classic example of someone who's always financially good to people and incredibly generous of spirit." Nonetheless, Clarke drew the line at living with her unpredictable boyfriend, preferring instead to maintain separate accommodation. "His flat is indescribable . . . like the flat in *The Young Ones*, only after it had been cleaned." MacGowan's North London dwelling has subsequently become the stuff of legend – a veritable wasteland of discarded cigarette packets, empty bottles, video cassettes (Sam Peckinpah and Sergio Leone movies are a particular favourite) and various scraps of paper filled with lyrics and chord structures. Whether he owns a Hoover remains a question for the gods . . .

Back in 1992, however, Shane was still content to lie low among the bottles and cartons while his former colleagues pressed ahead with the business of re-establishing their name. At the end of May, The Pogues released a rather grim version of The Rolling Stones' classic, 'Honky Tonk Women', backed by two further tunes: the compelling 'Infinity' and Jem Finer's bitter-sweet 'Curse Of Love' – a track originally presented to the band at the recording sessions for *Hell's Ditch* nearly two years before. In fact, The Pogues' snotty treatment of 'Honky Tonk Women' was also far from new, having first surfaced as the B-side to 'Yeah, Yeah, Yeah, Yeah, Yeah' in December, 1988. Yet, it remained an important addition to the group's catalogue, if only for the fact that '. . . Women' introduced the gruff strains of Spider Stacy to the Great British public. Having considered the possibility of Joe Strummer taking over as lead singer, The Pogues eventually decided to "promote from within", with Stacy stepping up to the microphone and Strummer returning to solo projects. Though the parting was entirely amicable, it was also somewhat confusing as Spider became the third Pogues' vocalist within the space of ten months. Still, the single performed adequately enough, peaking at number 56 on May 30.

By that time, the group were once again back on the road, making another headlining appearance at Finsbury Park's Fleadh festival with The Cranberries and Christy Moore in support. Faced with a crowd numbering twenty-odd thousand, Stacy proved himself an engaging enough frontman, using a combination of witty on-stage repartee and copious amounts of head-scratching to cover the occasional cracks in his voice. The highlight of the gig came predictably enough with Phil Chevron's 'Thousands Are Sailing', its message concerning the plight of Ireland's immigrant class ringing many a bell with those Celts in attendance. Backstage, the party continued, with a surprise guest popping in to wish the band well. Putting aside recent events, Shane MacGowan chatted briefly to his former colleagues before setting to work on the complimentary bar. Inevitably, his presence fuelled rumours that a reconciliation between both sides was imminent, but like most gossip, it all came to nought. The Pogues – minus Shane – performed at WOMAD's "10th Birthday Party" in Victoria Park, Bath on August 23, before commencing on a UK tour in the late autumn.

After nearly a year of considering his options, Shane finally returned to public view in November, 1992. Perhaps still reticent to present himself as a solo artist, he accepted an offer from fellow "child of the night" Nick Cave to record an unlikely cover version of jazz legend Louis Armstrong's 'What A Wonderful World'. Like MacGowan, Cave was something of a maverick talent, beginning his career as lead vocalist with the doom-laden Birthday Party in the early Eighties before forming his own band, The Bad Seeds, in 1984. Their first LP, *From Her To Eternity* set the style for all future excursions with the group's slow-moving harmonic lines providing a perfect backdrop for Cave's gravel-voiced tales of twisted love, gothic landscapes and, more often than not, murderous retribution. Subsequent album releases, such as *The First Born Is Dead, Tender Prey* and *Henry's Dream* only intensified the vocalist's image as a "dark troubadour", his penchant for dwelling on life's 'little atrocities' in lyric and song providing him an intensely devoted cult following.

MacGowan and Cave had been friends for some time, the two regularly bumping into each other at gigs and various TV shows. "I remember a long time ago The Pogues challenged The Birthday Party to a drinking competition," Nick recalled. "We turned up to the pub, (but) The Pogues chickened out. So we won by default . . ." On a more serious note, Shane actually

wrote 'House Of The Gods' (recorded on *Hell's Ditch*) with
Cave in mind, regarding the native Australian as one of the
few singers capable of doing justice to his work. "Me and him
have a lot in common," MacGowan said. "We both know how
to project – when we sing, people shut up . . ." Nick was quick
to return the compliment. "I'd wanted to do 'What A Wonderful World' for some time, and it just seemed an appropriate
duet to do with Shane – who's really one of my heroes."

On the face of it, 'What A Wonderful World' seemed an odd
choice for both Cave and MacGowan. In contrast to their
previous endeavours, the tune appeared to carry no dark
undercurrent at all, its lyrics positively extolling the joys of life.
Cave, however, remained unconvinced that '. . . World' was all
sweetness and light: "Shane wanted to work with me, and the
original idea was to do a few slow songs in the studio," he told
NME. "But (when) we went in, '. . . Wonderful World' came
very quickly. I'd always loved it, because behind the celebration of life, there's a real underbelly of sadness in Louis
Armstrong's version. This is a black man who had a lot of
problems. It's a melancholy song." Backed by Cave's rendition
of The Pogues' 'A Rainy Night In Soho', and a new MacGowan
composition, the doe-eyed 'Lucy', 'What A Wonderful World'
was released by Mute Records in the first week of December,
1992. Unfortunately, the single stalled at a lowly number 72,
falling out of the charts the following week. Despite its failure,
Shane remained philosophical when asked if he would work
with Cave again: "Maybe we'll do some more and maybe we
won't . . ."

In reality, MacGowan must have hoped for far more from
his collaboration with Nick Cave. If the single had broken the
Top 30, it would undoubtedly have re-activated interest in his
past and given him a springboard from which to launch a solo
career. Now, he was in danger of being relegated to the status
of minor celebrity – a performer whose best moments lay well
behind him. Thankfully, ZTT didn't see it that way. In fact,

word leaked out in January, 1993 that Jill Sinclair's record company had signed Shane. However, securing a new deal did little to temper the singer's enthusiasms, with MacGowan allegedly ingesting almost every substance known to man, beast or chemist. In addition to the alcohol, Shane's experimental nature had brought him into close proximity with ecstasy, speed and, even more worryingly, cocaine.

Though he chose not to confirm or deny the truth of such allegations, MacGowan remained firm on the question of LSD. "Yeah, it's true, I did do 50 tabs a day," he said, "but once you go over a few tabs, that's it . . . it doesn't have any further effect . . ." Thankfully, Shane was showing restraint in some areas of his life, having markedly changed his drinking habits following stern medical advice. Whiskey and brandy were strictly forbidden ("Brandy is the killer," he once said), and summarily replaced by white wine, king-sized measures of Martini, and the odd pint of Guinness – presumably drunk for variety rather than strength. In comparison to previous levels of intoxication, he was now almost sober: "My liver is regenerating," MacGowan offered at the time . . .

As Shane doused himself in anticipation of the future, The Pogues announced their return in August, 1993 with a new single – 'Tuesday Morning'. Written by Spider Stacy, the song was something of a surprise for older fans, more resembling straight-ahead soft rock than traditional folk. However, 'Tuesday Morning' remained a pleasing little tune, its chugging chorus recalling the likes of John Waite's 1987 hit 'Missing You': "But I knew," sang a misty-eyed Stacy, "that you, with your heart beating and your eyes shining, would be dreaming of me . . ." Immediately picked up by radio, 'Tuesday Morning' gave The Pogues their first Top 20 hit since 1988, the song acting as an able advertisement for the group's forthcoming LP, *Waiting For Herb*. Sadly, when the album finally arrived in stores, it proved somewhat less interesting than its intriguing title suggested, being a largely uneven collection of sentimental ballads, wobbly Middle-Eastern folk turns and straight ahead rockers. In short, *Waiting For Herb* was better than the woeful *Hell's Ditch*, perhaps even on a par with *Peace And Love*, but not a patch on *Rum, Sodomy And The Lash* or *If I Should Fall From Grace With God*.

That said, there were some genuinely thrilling moments on show. Terry Wood's uptempo ghost story, 'Haunting', allowed The Pogues to re-visit their Irish traditional roots in fine style, while James Fearnley's 'Drunken Boat' introduced a distinctly French flavour to proceedings, with accordions, clarinets and soprano saxophones all fighting for musical supremacy: "Mother, pack my bags because I'm off to foreign ports," went Fearnley's deft lyric. "Don't ask me where I'm going 'cause I'm sure it's off the charts . . ." But the biggest surprise on *Waiting For Herb* surely had to be drummer Andrew Ranken's vocal début on 'My Baby's Gone'. Coming over as a cross between Howling Wolf and a particularly angry Tom Waits, Ranken's growling tones set light to an otherwise average rock song, casting serious doubt on whether The Pogues had picked the right singer to replace Shane MacGowan. It was a point not lost on music critics.

"Frankly, Spider's voice, though appropriately tough in smallish doses, can't carry a whole LP," reasoned *NME*'s Danny Frost, "and he struggles with Shane's legacy of inspired sentimentality. (Yet), the least of *Waiting For Herb*'s numerous disappointments is its lack of Shane MacGowan. We were still entitled to expect much, much more – more focus, more guts, more songs . . . please start again." *Q*'s Sid Griffin was some-what more forgiving of The Pogues' latest offering. Yet, even he could not raise the flag of support above half-mast. "*Waiting For Herb* resembles nothing so much as Beach Boys albums after Brian Wilson let go the reins – post *Smile*," wrote Griffin. "If there are no new readily identifiable Pogues classics here, there are also no real clunkers, leaving *Waiting For Herb* as dis-tinctly transitional."

All in all, it was a fair point. No one could realistically expect The Pogues to deliver a classic LP so soon after dispensing with MacGowan's services. The group needed time to re-evaluate their position and focus on which direction to take. Sadly, they also had to face up to several uncomfortable truths. For one, no matter how likeable a character Spider Stacy was, his voice lacked the bark (and bite) of their former frontman. If The Pogues were to survive and prosper, they might well have to re-consider their choice of vocalist altogether. More tellingly, Shane's dismissal had left the group with a glaring hole in their songwriting department. While Jem Finer could partially be relied upon to fill in the gaps, his natural predilection for penning ballads meant *Waiting For Herb* was a far more sedate LP than any of its predecessors – no bad thing perhaps, if the material on show was comparable to previous glories such as 'Fairytale Of New York' or 'Misty Morning, Albert Bridge'. But 'Once Upon A Time' and 'Small Hours' were little more than dull approximations of those fine tunes. In the cold light of day, The Pogues' weaknesses were now starting to outweigh their strengths.

Produced by Michael Brook (the inventor of the 'Infinite Guitar' system), *Waiting For Herb* made a momentary appearance at number 20 in the UK albums chart before swiftly disappearing into the bargain bins. For Terry Woods and James Fearnley, the LP's relative failure signalled a natural end to their career with the band, the pair leaving almost simultaneously in the late autumn of 1993 (a disenchanted Phil Chevron would soon follow). Down, but not quite out, Stacy, Finer, Ranken and Hunt decided to soldier on, recruiting new boys James McNally, David Coulter and Jamie Clarke on accordion, mandolin and guitar respectively. A suitable baptism of fire was provided for the trio at Kentish Town's Forum club on December 20, when Shane MacGowan joined his old band on stage to perform rousing versions 'The Irish Rover' and the anthemic 'Streams Of Whiskey'. To add to the air of familiarity, Joe Strummer also showed up for the gig, bashing his way through a particularly virulent rendition of 'I Fought The Law'. As with Fleadh '91, Shane's presence at The Forum led to various rumours that he was about to re-join The Pogues, with one music paper even going as far as to suggest that his imminent return had caused Woods and Fearnley to quit the group.

In some ways, the stories were true. MacGowan was about to return to the fray. Yet, it was on his own terms and with his own agenda. In fact, the irascible singer was about to pull off an almost Lazarus-like resurrection many thought wholly beyond him.

FIFTEEN

The Dead Arose And Appeared To Many

Since being asked to leave The Pogues in September, 1991, Shane MacGowan had enjoyed a largely carefree existence. Aside from negotiating a new record deal with ZTT and laying down the odd vocal with Nick Cave, he was content to spend his time travelling, seeing old friends and family and having the odd drink. Ever ready to indulge his love of all things Irish, MacGowan temporarily moved to the outskirts of Dublin, staying first as a guest at Bono's opulent Martello Tower (a property the singer owned in Bray), before upping sticks to a rented flat in Mountjoy Square in the heart of the city. Using Ireland's capital as a base of operations, Shane was able to make frequent trips to his childhood home of North West Tipperary, some ninety miles away. All in all, it made for an idyllic existence.

However, there was the odd hiccup along the way. In September, 1993, for instance, Shane was enjoying a relatively quiet night at Bad Bob's bar in central Dublin, when fellow reveller (and long-term Dublin resident) Lisa Stansfield took major exception to his lack of social skills. Having made several failed attempts to engage the former Pogue in conversation, the soul singer – best known for her chart topping 1989 hit 'All Around The World' – decided to move things along by striking MacGowan square on the nose. Fortunately for the pub's other guests, which included Van Morrison and The

158

Hothouse Flowers' Fiacra O'Braonain, Shane chose not to retaliate. As with the "cannibalism incident" all those years ago at the ICA, initial reports indicated MacGowan's nose was broken in the fracas. This time, it was true. "Blood everywhere," said an aggrieved Shane . . .

Yet, whatever the damage inflicted, Stansfield's assault seemed to trigger something in MacGowan as he became progressively more active in the months that followed. In fact, by the winter of 1993, he confirmed his new, as yet unnamed band would be on the road within four months. At first, these proclamations were given short shrift by the musical intelligentsia who, like many of his fans, seriously doubted MacGowan's ability to reclaim former glories. After all, the man dismissed by The Pogues some two years before was, by his own admission, "less than fighting fit" and, as recent sightings confirmed, he seemed more interested in drinking his way around the capital cities of the world than actually playing in them. In short, the popular perception of Shane was "damaged goods" – a great talent perhaps, but one unlikely to return from the Twilight Zone into which he had knowingly consigned himself.

Like the horse he immortalised in 'Bottle Of Smoke', MacGowan came from the back to prove the bookies wrong. The first stirrings of renewed activity came in February, 1994, when a surprisingly passive Shane duetted alongside Van Morrison at the annual Brit Awards. On the back of that appearance, it was announced that he was to play a concert at the Clapham Grand on St. Patrick's Night a month later. As critics sharpened their pencils in anticipation of his return, Shane simply stated it "would be a night to remember . . ." He wasn't wrong. In fact, MacGowan's 'gig at the Grand' turned out to be one of the more enjoyable events of the year, receiving rave reviews from all corners of the music press (serious or otherwise), as well as delighting those in attendance.

Taking the stage dressed in his now trademark black, Shane

completed his ensemble with wraparound shades, a large silver crucifix and a spacious gap where his front teeth used to be. His hair too, had undergone fundamental change. Once content to obey the laws of gravity, it now shot up from his head towards the ceiling in quite astonishing fashion. In short, he looked every inch the rock star. The only remaining question was whether he had the goods to back up the image. Thankfully, MacGowan didn't disappoint, offering a spirited performance that drew on every aspect of his musical career. Beginning the set with 'Streams Of Whiskey', he plundered his own Pogues back catalogue to fine, sonorous effect, before pulling out a few choice surprises as the night wore on.

The Nipple Erectors' signature tune, 'King Of The Bop', returned to his repertoire after a fourteen year absence as well as an intense re-working of 1987's 'If I Should Fall From Grace With God'. After several 'head-crushers', Shane radically dropped the pace by introducing Nick Cave from the wings to duet with him on a showy rendition of Frank Sinatra's 'Love's Been Good To Me'. Following that little manoeuvre, he re-activated his former pace before ushering sister Siobhan on stage to sing Kirsty MacColl's part on an emotive treatment of 'Fairytale Of New York'. With a final blast of 'The Irish Rover', MacGowan took his bows and was gone again.

The St. Patrick's Night show at the Clapham Grand proved that Shane was surely capable of re-invigorating himself if he tried hard enough. In stark contrast to the sorry figure who shambled onto the stage only three years before, he now seemed brimful of confidence, content to regale his audience with a heady mixture of past glories and future intent. MacGowan had assembled a brand new band, cheekily christened The Popes. And what a rum lot they were too. All scruffy T-shirts, drainpipe jeans and matted beards, The Popes more resembled a group of stranded pirates than men accorded the responsibility of bringing Shane's latest batch of rebel songs to life. Yet they had major form. Comprising Paul McGuiness (guitar and backing vocals), Bernie 'The Undertaker' France (bass), Kieran 'Mo' O'Hagan (rhythm guitar), Colm O'Maonlai (whistles), Danny Pope (drums) and the fiercely named Tom MacAnimal (tenor banjo), each musician could call on years of experience in both the studio and on stage. A far more aggressive prospect than Shane's previous act, The Popes also had little truck with the niceties of acoustic instrumentation, preferring instead to plug in, turn up and "see what happens". "What this band is all about," reasoned Danny, "is Irish roots and Irish rock'n'roll . . ."

MacGowan and The Popes had spent much of February rehearsing at a tiny studio near Pentonville Prison, before finally playing some warm up gigs in Dublin and Harlesden's Mean Fiddler (in anticipation of their official début at the Clapham Grand). The group was surprised that MacGowan turned out to be such a harsh taskmaster. "He's definitely a musical dictator," Danny later confirmed to *Rock 'n' Reel*. To Shane, however, it was his reputation, and not theirs, that was on the line. "The Popes are a backing band," he stated emphatically. "I write the songs, decide the songs we play, do the arrangements and produce the records." Obviously, there was the odd concession to be made. "When I'm in a band," MacGowan confirmed, "everybody's decision is taken into account. (Besides), they all happen to be friends of mine. There's no point in playing with musicians you don't get on with, because you don't have any chemistry." What the group specifically brought to Shane was a punk spirit criminally lacking in his recordings since 1987's *If I Should Fall From Grace With God*. A loud, abrasive six-man unit, The Popes were both a catalyst and conduit for MacGowan's dormant energies, allowing him the luxury of re-visiting his past, taking pride in his victories and then dragging them – kicking and screaming – into the present.

Shuddering proof of this came in September, 1994 with the release of Shane and The Popes' first single, 'Church Of The

161

Holy Spook'. Brimful of evangelical zeal, '. . . Spook' was
MacGowan's latest call to arms – its wrenching beat and metal-
lic guitars providing the perfect backdrop for a self-referential
tale of rock'n'roll martyrdom. "Rock'n'roll, you crucified me,
left me all alone . . ." Though Shane was at pains to point out
the song wasn't directly autobiographical, '. . . Spook' still
managed to champion his religious beliefs, namechecking
both Catholicism and Taoism within the space of three short
minutes. "I believe in the church of the holy spook . . . the Tao
is like a river, so float along with me . . ." "I'm a Catholic Taoist
hedonist," MacGowan revealed at the time, "I'm (also) a lapsed
Catholic, but I wouldn't go anywhere without my crucifix. I'm
frightened of vampires. There's enough of them about . . ." A
marvellous single, made all the more intriguing by Shane's
melding of Eastern philosophy with images of a suffering
Jesus, 'Church Of The Holy Spook' nevertheless performed
disappointingly in the charts, stuttering to a halt at a lowly
number 72. Evidently, it was time to bring in the big guns.

MacGowan's secret weapon arrived at Heathrow Airport
from Los Angeles on Tuesday, September 27, 1994 in the
unlikely form of Johnny Depp. Once described by critic/
comedian Jonathan Ross as "the coolest man in the universe",
Depp personified a new breed of Hollywood actor who chose
film roles that genuinely interested him rather than vehicles
designed to raise his public profile. Depp graduated from TV
cop drama *21 Jump Street* in the late Eighties, but his penchant
for dating beautiful starlets (*Dirty Dancing*'s Jennifer Grey,
Twin Peaks' Sherilyn Fenn and, most notably, Oscar-nominated
actress Winona Ryder) often overshadowed his real worth on
the screen. Fine performances in movies such as *Cry Baby* and
the surreal fairytale *Edward Scissorhands* tended to be overshadowed by news of his latest romantic liaison. Though Depp
repeatedly tried to deflect attention away from his love-life, a
high-profile romance with British supermodel Kate Moss had
recently dragged his features onto the front page. "Whether

Kate Moss and I are together is nobody's business but mine or hers," he growled in late 1993. "I'd rather the press wrote that I'm fucking dogs than rely on them to write anything real about our relationship . . ."

Away from the incessant media coverage, Depp was quite the fan of rock'n'roll, actually beginning his climb to fame in the early Eighties as lead guitarist with The Kids, a Florida-based act who went on to tour with Iggy Pop, amongst others. While the band split soon after re-locating to LA, where Johnny went on to pursue his career in movies, he remained an avid follower of music, even going as far as to open his own club, The Viper Room, in early 1994. Depp first crossed paths with Shane MacGowan on a lightning trip across the Atlantic. "I first met Shane in London," Depp recalled. "He was in the studio, sitting on a pool table with a guitar. I said 'Hello', so did he and that was that. It was . . . brief." After several further meetings, the two struck up a firm friendship. "I was in bands before I ever started the other thing," said Johnny. "I was a musician for years and years and had always been a fan of The Pogues and Shane's lyrics." For MacGowan, it all boiled down to common interests. "Johnny's a musician, I'm a musician, we're mates, so it's all kinda natural . . ."

When Shane began the process of recording his first solo album, he cordially extended an invitation to Depp to appear on it. Suitably flattered, Johnny arrived at the studio with guitar in hand. According to MacGowan, a fine night was had by all. "Johnny's playing was a bit erratic – very good – but it wasn't always anything to do with the track he was playing along with. So we mixed it around a bit, you know what I mean? You can hear bits of Johnny if you listen very carefully. But unless you were down there, paying attention . . . and Johnny definitely wasn't . . . it'd be hard to say which bits are Johnny and which bits aren't. We were," he concluded, "all pretty out of it . . ." The track in question, a violently paced rocker entitled 'That Woman's Got Me Drinking' was subsequently chosen as Shane's second single from his forthcoming LP.

To promote its release, Depp flew in to appear with MacGowan on *Top Of The Pops*. Yet, from the moment his feet hit the tarmac, the actor was actively pursued by the press, eager no doubt, to learn more about his relationship with Kate Moss. Though Johnny was well used to the attention, Shane grew increasingly irritated by the constant intrusions on his friend's time. "Everybody was trying to get an angle on it," MacGowan told *Q*. "My record company, the papers. I was more pissed off than he was . . ." In the end, it was all worth it, with Shane and Johnny combining their talents to produce an anarchic three minutes of TV. "She said she'd always love me," MacGowan howled into camera, ". . . said I was the one . . . look at the way she treats me, like a piece of scum."

Johnny Depp's contributions didn't end with his *Top Of The Pops* appearance. After filming concluded, he, MacGowan and The Popes were whisked across London to the Elephant And Castle to shoot a straightforward performance video for the song. "We got a perfectly good video," Shane quipped. "It took about an hour to do – which seems short – but it's not a very long record." This promo for 'That Woman's Got Me Drinking' was actually the second one produced – the original video (directed by Depp) – being deemed too controversial for prime-time viewing. "I was talking on the phone with Shane," Johnny later confirmed, "and he asked me did I want to (direct) the video and, of course, I jumped at the chance. Two days later, we were shooting." In Depp's version, he cast himself as a talkative drunk while Shane played the sober, disinterested barman, forced to listen to Johnny's vocal outbursts. While the role reversal worked well enough, several scenes featuring excessive smoking/drinking meant TV stations couldn't air the clip before "the 9 p.m. watershed". An "in-concert" rendition of the tune was therefore necessary for earlier transmission and this was hastily concocted at the Elephant.

In the days that followed, MacGowan and Depp spent their time "knocking around London" before the actor returned to work in Los Angeles. There can be no question that Johnny's fleeting visit to British shores had done untold good for Shane's public profile. Cool once again (albeit by association), MacGowan found himself back in the UK charts at a reasonable number 34 with 'That Woman's Got Me Drinking', and therefore in pole position to release his new album. On October 29, 1994, the waiting was finally over.

SIXTEEN

Crawling From The Wreckage

Shane MacGowan's first solo LP, *The Snake*, effectively condensed sixteen years of songwriting experience into some fifty-six minutes of recorded material. An album of extremes, whose charms ranged from country music and Irish traditional folk to raggedly assured rock'n'roll, *The Snake* presented MacGowan as an artist with much left to say about the world around him, even if those observations were made from the bottom of a pint glass. Though Shane would later dismiss it as "an atrocity", *The Snake* remains strangely compelling – a flawed, yet fascinating collection of songs documenting one man's stubborn refusal to "go quietly into the good night".

Of the compositions MacGowan chose to present, there were several obvious highlights. Aside from the singles 'Church Of The Holy Spook' and the bruising grandeur of 'That Woman's Got Me Drinking', both 'A Mexican Funeral In Paris' and 'I'll Be Your Handbag' proved Shane could still wreak havoc with three spare chords, the latter tune almost taking up where The Nips left off. "Skinheads, coppers, they're all cock-suckers . . . me, I'm recovering from a nine day drunk." Elsewhere, MacGowan upheld his interest in covering old Irish rebel songs, the lyrics to 'Roddy McCorley' and 'The Rising Of The Moon' positively awash with Republican imagery. "All along that singing river a black mass of men was seen, and above their shining weapons hung their own beloved green . . . death to every foe and traitor!"

Nonetheless, there was still a romantic's heart beating beneath all the battle armour. In 'You're The One', for instance, Shane constructed (with the assistance of classical composer Michael Kamen) a quite exquisite ballad, made all the more affecting by the presence of Clannad's Máire Brennan on shared lead vocals. "Funny how the circle turns," crooned MacGowan. "Funny how the flame still burns," came Brennan's singular reply. Despite its obvious worth, 'You're The One' failed to chart when released as a single in June, 1995. A song that fared considerably better with the public was Shane's soft-rocking duet with Sinéad O'Connor, the lilting 'Haunted'. Though melodically inferior to 'You're The One', 'Haunted' was carried along by the pleasing juxtaposition of O'Connor's angelic tones and MacGowan's gravel-like tenor. "I saw you standing in the street," croaked a not so misty-eyed Shane. "You were so cool, you could have put out Vietnam . . ." Marking the beginning of a "beautiful friendship" between the two (they would subsequently fall out in quite spectacular fashion some five years later), 'Haunted' reached number 30 in the UK in April, 1995.

Tucked away amongst all these ballads and battle-cries were three of *The Snake*'s more interesting moments: 'Victoria', 'The Snake With The Eyes Of Garnet' and a sneaky little tune named 'Aisling'. In the case of 'Victoria', MacGowan was in remarkably candid form, verbally flagellating himself after his long-suffering girlfriend, Victoria Clarke, chose to end their relationship. "My girl with green eyes is no longer beside me." Evidently, his enduring love affair with Class A substances had driven the remarkably patient Clarke out the door. "I'll put my pipe aside and hit the road . . ." Thankfully, the pair later reconciled their differences. If 'Victoria' presented a more vulnerable side to Shane's character, then 'The Snake With Eyes Of Garnet' announced the welcome return of the rebel poet. As with 'Streams Of Whiskey' all those years before, 'The

Snake . . .' found MacGowan being led through a dream by another of his literary heroes, Republican bard James Mangan. Yet, this time Shane is presented with a magic talisman (the snake of the title), with the power to protect its owner. "This snake cannot be tortured, or hung or crucified . . ."

A time-travelling tale of doomed convicts, drunken troubadours and more than a little witchcraft, 'The Snake With The Eyes Of Garnet' remains interesting not only for its quasi-spiritual undertones, but also for re-introducing the name James Mangan to a contemporary audience: "He was a Republican, an alcoholic, a junkie. He didn't care and he died young (because of it)," MacGowan later confirmed to the BBC. "I'm an admirer of the way he lived his life . . . it's something I can identify with, you know. Of course, I'd always put my health first, as painful as that might be . . ." A native Dubliner, renowned as much for his support of Republicanism as his way with words, James Mangan died in 1849 at the age of 46.

Another of MacGowan's compositions, 'Aisling', also owed a clear debt to Mangan, albeit in more prosaic terms. By way of explanation, during the height of British influence in Ireland, all expressions of nationalistic fervour were duly banned. This situation forced Eire's poets and songwriters to mask any tribute to their country, or its fight for independence, in obscure verse. Therefore, Ireland became 'a young woman in a loveless marriage' or 'a flowing river seeking escape into the sea', the image of a nation under siege constantly repressed in ever more beautiful imagery. The most famous of these "vision poems", or to give them their Gaelic name "Aislings", was James Mangan's 'Roisin Dœbh', more popularly known as 'Dark Rosaleen' or 'Black Rose'. Interested in both resurrecting the form and paying due tribute to Mangan, Shane wrote his own 'Aisling' in 1989. However, The Pogues rejected the song, so he duly handed it over to another of his heroes, ex-Planxty frontman and "resident Irish treasure" Christy

Moore. In truth, Moore still performs a better version of the tune, his jaunty acoustic style enlivening MacGowan's original lyric to great effect. That said, the treatment of 'Aisling' on *The Snake* is not without its charms, its melody propelled along on the back of some fine drumming and suspiciously familiar penny whistle/banjo interludes.

As with anything Shane put his name to, *The Snake* courted its fair share of controversy. Aside from some critical rumblings about the number of Republican-themed tunes present on the LP, there were persistent allegations that MacGowan "appropriated" the melody from Paul Brady's 'The Homes Of Donegal' for his own tender ballad, 'The Song With No Name'. Whether true or not (and it is unlikely), 'The Song With No Name' numbered among Shane's finest ever creations, its portrayal of a man forcing away his one true love cutting to the emotional quick. "I was brutal . . . ignorant . . . cruel . . . brash . . . I never gave a damn about the beauty that I smashed." Aside from the odd cry of "theft", MacGowan also had to put up with some barracking from fans of Van Morrison, who took issue with an unflattering portrayal of their hero in the lyrics to 'Victoria'. "Victoria left me in opium euphoria, with a fat monk singing 'Gloria'." The clear reference to one of Morrison's theme songs was undoubtedly meant as a joke, but legend has it that 'The Man' himself was less than pleased with Shane's moving tribute to his waistline . . .

Produced by MacGowan and Dave Jordan, an ex-Pogues soundman (and unaccredited producer of 'A Rainy Night In Soho'), *The Snake* took the term 'guest musician' to new limits, with a veritable legion of pals – both old and new – lining up to appear on it. Aside from the contributions of Johnny Depp, Sinéad O'Connor and Máire Brennan, both Spider Stacy and Jem Finer lent Shane a hand on 'Aisling'. Thin Lizzy guitarist extraordinaire Brian Robertson also popped up "here and there", as did The Dubliners' Barney McKenna and John Sheahan. When one included the session talents of Siobhan

Sheahan, Tomas Lynch, Dick Cuthell, Paul Taylor, Rick Trevan and Sarah Jane Tuff alongside MacGowan's resident backing band The Popes, the combined total of artists contributing to *The Snake* numbered 20 in all. With so much time and effort gone into the album, it was perhaps unsurprising when *The Snake* received almost blanket adoration from the rock press.

"*The Snake* sees MacGowan nailed up on the cross for mistaking rock'n'roll for religion, searching for Christ and an errant woman with green eyes," said *Melody Maker*'s Cathi Unsworth. "Shane, like any hero worth having, is a lover, a fighter, a wild bull rider, always there to sock you between the eyes with the living truth that created his scars . . . here are more songs to astound and amaze, to drink from holy chalices and stained beer glasses, until the end of the world." *Mojo*'s David Cavanagh also couldn't get enough of *The Snake*'s charms. "Plenty of great new songs, Irish sounding ones ('The Snake With Eyes Of Garnet' and 'Aisling') and frenetic, slam-drunk rock'n'roll roof-raisers ('The Church Of The Holy Spook', 'That Woman's Got Me Drinking' and 'I'll Be Your Handbag'). Not even Nick Cave has sung so enthusiastically of heroin, opium and drink while professing to get better. Yet, *The Snake*, for all its dark ands violent imagery is never an uncomfortable listen . . . MacGowan is now marked down as a survivor . . . and The Snake (is) a superior rock-Irish record."

For all the attendant praise, *The Snake* wasn't without its faults. While MacGowan was to be commended for revisiting his punk roots in songs such as 'I'll Be Your Handbag', howling lyrical protest at skinheads and police somewhat dated the ferocity of his attack, things having clearly moved on since the clashes of 1976. Additionally, years of self-abuse had sadly compromised Shane's voice, the full-throated roar present on *Rum, Sodomy And The Lash* now replaced by a smokey growl. Sometimes the change in intonation worked, as with 'That Woman's Got Me Drinking' and 'The Song With

No Name', but on tunes such as 'A Mexican Funeral In Paris' and 'Nancy Whiskey', MacGowan sounded plain tired, seemingly content to limp his way through the lyrics rather than sing them. Still, for a man declared "all but dead" by the press only three years before, any sound exiting from his mouth was cause enough for celebration.

Despite the odd glitch, *The Snake* remained a fine album, allowing its creator to confront and confound his critics, and move past the unposted obituary that spelled the end of his career with The Pogues. Yet, the LP only achieved moderate sales, peaking at number 37 in the UK on October 29, 1994, before completely falling out of the charts two weeks later. At the time MacGowan stood defiant, but by 1997, his opinion of *The Snake* had radically soured. "It's a mess," he said. "Basically, it's a rock record . . . an atrocity. Three or four good tracks and the rest of it is rubbish." Back in 1994, however, it was "rubbish" in need of drastic promotion. Though he professed to despise the process, Shane MacGowan once again hit the road.

SEVENTEEN

You Liver And Learn

"I've drunk to your health in the taverns, I've drunk to
   your health in my home,
I've drunk to your health so many times, I've almost
   ruined my own . . ."

— saying found on Irish tea towel.

Since Shane MacGowan last troubled the charts in the winter
of 1992, great changes had occurred within the UK music
scene. After promising much, the 'Madchester' movement
that spawned bands such as Happy Mondays and The Stone
Roses was now on its last legs, irrevocably compromised by the
wayward behaviour of its principal players. Eager to fill the
vacuum generated by Madchester's demise, the press was busy
building up hype around a new generation of British groups.
Though they shared precious little in common, acts such as
Blur, Oasis, Pulp, Shed Seven and Menswear found themselves
wrapped together in a soothing blanket named 'Britpop', a
generic term conferred on all those young, feather-haired
musicians who expressed even the vaguest interest in The
Beatles, The Small Faces or anyone else holding a guitar
or banging a drum throughout the Sixties. By mid 1994,
'Britpop' escaped from the pages of the music papers and
found its way into the hearts and minds of British youth, the

success of Blur's *Parklife* and Oasis' *Definitely Maybe* signalling a new era of Union Jack scooters, Fred Perry tops and ill-fitting Parka jackets.

Whether MacGowan knew or even cared about this latest shift in Great Britain's cultural fortunes remains uncertain. Having embarked on a truly stupendous "lost weekend" that saw him disappear from public view for the best part of three years, it seems a safe bet to suggest that he remained 'uninterested'. Certainly, there was precious little evidence on *The Snake* to suggest that Shane had spent time listening to old Kinks records or re-visiting The Beatles' back catalogue for musical inspiration. On the contrary, he'd turned to a more staple diet of punk, country and Irish traditional folk to fuel his creative engine. Yet, MacGowan's complete disavowal of anything constituting a trend meant his appeal remained limited to an already established following – a fact reflected in the modest sales accorded his latest disc. Of course, at the age of 37, it would have been both unsightly and undignified for him to try and compete with pop's young lions, yet recording *The Snake* had proved an expensive business. To ensure a return on his investment, he had to drum up the interest of the media in his wares and, equally as important, recapture those stray fans who grew tired awaiting his return.

As ever, MacGowan found little difficulty in courting the press. Though he was known as "a difficult interview", he remained one of the few performers who could truly say they had "tried just about everything". In fact, with the possible exception of The Rolling Stones' Keith Richards (a man once described as having a face "more lined than a Southern region rail map"), MacGowan was unequalled in his excesses, the evidence writ large in every bar from Bangkok to Dublin. To put it bluntly, what Shane MacGowan hadn't done simply wasn't worth talking about. But what he had certainly was. That fact alone made him an alluring prospect. To compound journalistic delight, the ex-Pogue was also exceedingly blunt in his views, with little or no truck for diplomacy, brinkmanship or witty repartee. When asked a question, he simply answered it. Unless of course, his inquisitor was given to needless flights of intellectual whimsy, in which case, Shane simply told them to "Fuck off, or start again . . ."

Predictably then, little time was spent discussing the allegorical symbolism of 'the Snake', or its enduring connection to Ireland's religious history when MacGowan met with the press in the late autumn of 1994. Instead, enquiries largely focused on the state of his health and whether the rumours concerning drugs, drink and, in probability, industrial effluent had any credence. Never one to run from the truth, Shane hit hard and low. "Listen, I'm not a healthy man," he told *Loaded*'s Jon Wilde. "I've lived a totally irresponsible existence. I've given no thought to what I've swallowed, poured down my throat or stuck up my nose over the years. It was only when a doctor told me I was like a cat running out of lives that I decided to calm down . . . purely for the sake of staying alive. I've had to re-adjust to a slower pace and that's made writing more difficult. But I am recovering, starting to regenerate. Let's just say I've learned my lessons. You liver and learn."

Such rampant experimentation had a price though, with MacGowan reluctantly admitting to selling his collection of Pogues silver and gold discs to fund an escalating drug habit. "I flogged mine to a collector's shop and got a decent price," he confirmed to *Q.* "I was sensible. I'm sure Spider sold his for about fifty quid."

All in all, Shane's bluntness was like a breath of fresh air compared to the guarded admissions of many of his contemporaries. Yet, one had to worry. Having explored every nook and cranny of his constitution for the best part of three decades, there was always the risk his body might stage a bloody revolt, leading to prolonged hospitalisation or worse. Again MacGowan had an answer. "I'm a big boy," he grinned, "I know what I'm doing . . ." Still, subsequent appearances on *The Danny Baker Show* and *Later With Jools Holland* only intensified the level of interest in Shane's health, his habit of taking long pauses between words and sentences leading to confused laughter from the audience. Nevertheless, Shane always made for an entertaining guest, albeit one who more often than not spent rather too long in the hospitality lounge before the show and probably afterwards too.

Regardless of MacGowan's various proclivities, his media blitz ensured packed houses for a short tour he and The Popes embarked upon in November, 1994 – the undoubted high-light of which was two sold out nights at Kentish Town's Forum club. As with the Clapham Grand six months before, the sets proved fast and furious affairs, all jagged guitars and breakneck drumming. In standard fashion, Shane led from the front: hostile one moment, meek the next. "The gigs I most enjoy," he once said, "are the ones where I'm so angry and paranoid . . . when I hate the audience so much, that I put everything into it and feed off the aggressive side of it. I don't actually hate the fans, but when I'm feeling angry, pissed off and full of hate . . . it's a good gig for me." To mark his return to the stage, ZTT issued another single – the lovely '. . . Song With No Name' – just in time for Christmas. Unfortunately, it failed to chart.

Seemingly undeterred, MacGowan again tried his luck in April, 1995 with 'Haunted'. As previously revealed, the duet with Sinéad O'Connor finally saw him back in the UK Top 30 after an absence of nearly seven years. Evidently, its success was worth celebrating because aside from an anarchic appear-ance at Fleadh '95 and a few select gigs around Europe (including the Montreux Jazz Festival), Shane all but dis-appeared from public view for the rest of the year.

Fans could partially console themselves, however, with the return of his former group The Pogues, who released their seventh studio album, *Pogue Mahone,* in September, 1995. Given its self-referential title, one could only expect a 'back to basics' approach from MacGowan's erstwhile colleagues. And thankfully, that's exactly what they provided, the songs on *Pogue Mahone* often recalling the glory days of *Rum, Sodomy And The Lash* and *If I Should Fall From Grace With God.* As usual, Jem Finer was behind several of the finer tunes, with 'Bright Lights', 'Oretown' and the charming 'Tosspint' all particularly worthy of mention. Yet, he faced serious competition from the newly formed songwriting team of Daryll Hunt and James McNally, whose anthemic 'Living In A World Without Her' constituted three or so minutes of undiluted listening pleasure.

Elsewhere, Andrew Ranken also proved himself a fine tunesmith, handing in "a real shinkicker" entitled 'Amadie', as well as the mournful ballad 'Four O'Clock In The Morning'. Even Spider Stacy's voice – once so indistinct – had improved with time and constant touring, his rasping tones considerably warming up otherwise faithful cover versions of Bob Dylan's 'When The Ship Comes In' and Ronnie Lane's 'How Come'. Overall then, *Pogue Mahone* was almost as good as Shane MacGowan's . . . *Snake.* Sadly, it remains the "Great lost Pogues album", principally because next to nobody bought it. Weakened (in media terms at least) by the absence of Shane and struggling to find an audience outside the devoted few who stuck with them after 1993's disappointing *Waiting For Herb,* The Pogues were considered at best an anachronism, or at worst a historical oddity whose clock was rapidly running down.

Stubborn to a fault, the group battled on a while longer, playing two Christmas shows at the Shepherd's Bush Empire in December, 1995 before once again veering off to Europe for further live committments. However, following a set at the Montreux Jazz Festival on July 19, 1996, an announcement was made to the press that The Pogues were finally "calling it a day". Two weeks later, they performed their final gig – a low-key event, held unsurprisingly, in the back room of a London pub. Of the founding members, only three remained. To mark the occasion, Shane joined them for a number or two, before returning once again to his seat. Proving times don't really change, he almost managed to get himself thrown out of the bar earlier in the evening by the group's minders, who completely failed to recognise their distinguished charge. "It was," MacGowan concluded, "a misunderstanding."

Questioned about the demise of The Pogues, Shane was in no mood for tears. "I didn't feel anything about them breaking up. They've had nothing to do with me for a long time. I never understood why people thought they'd outlast me." By 1998, the milk had truly soured. "They've been living off my royalties for six years," MacGowan growled to *Irish Voice*. "I wrote most of the songs, apart from the traditional ones. I wanted to do *more* traditional ones. But the songs they wrote weren't really up to scratch . . . well, most of them. I mean, there were some classics, like (Phil Chevron's) 'Thousands Are Sailing', but in the end, we all hated each other. They hated me anyway . . ."

It was, perhaps, an uncharitable view. At their best, The Pogues were a grand collective of musicians, each excelling at their appointed task. Gifted, unpretentious and entertaining, the band were responsible for hauling Irish traditional folk off the comfy chair it had grown used to throughout the Seventies and re-introducing it to booze, expletives and the occasional fist fight. MacGowan had been at the heart of things – no sane mind could deny that. But without the likes of Finer, Stacy, Fearnley and Ranken, his dream of "going all the way" might have taken a radically different form. Or indeed, come to naught. When asked in 1985 what he wanted The Pogues to be remembered for, Shane offered the following: "I'd like to say we reflected reality without being deliberately miserable, or offering unobtainable escapism." But Andrew Ranken may have come somewhat closer to forever defining the group's peculiar appeal. "The Pogues? Agony and ecstasy . . . and everything in between."

As The Pogues consigned themselves to musical history,

MacGowan was again back in the charts with a touching, if somewhat deranged version of that old Sinatra chestnut, 'My Way'. In many ways, it was the perfect song for him to cover, its lyrical tale of one man coming out ahead in spite of life's little foibles providing a fine vehicle for Shane to indulge his sense of irony. Indeed, as he wrapped his cigarette-stained vocal cords around that immortal phrase "I've lived a life that's full, and travelled each and every highway . . . and more, much more than this, I did it my way," it was almost impossible not to raise a wry smile. Backed by 'The Song With No Name' and 'Aisling', 'My Way' reached number 30 in the early summer of 1996. To swell MacGowan's bank account even further, the tune was picked up by sporting giants Nike – acting as background music for a TV advertisement promoting their latest range of Swoosh trainers. Whether Shane was ever approached by the company to run around a track wearing their shoes remains uncertain, but one could hazard a guess as to his probable response . . .

All in all then, 1996 was a good year for MacGowan. Against expectation, he had seen off his former rivals (even going so far as to attend their wake), pushed himself back onto *Top Of The Pops* at the ripe old age of thirty nine and even gone as far as announcing plans for the release of a second solo album in 1997. Though no one would blame him for kicking up his feet and gloating over a job well done, Shane chose instead to see out the year with two sterling performances at Dublin's Olympia theatre on December 21/22. From there, it was a short journey south towards Tipperary and Christmas with his family. "Ireland's my home," he later told *Rock 'n' Reel*'s Charmaine O'Reilly. "It always was. I just love getting on the boat, it makes me happy. When I left school at fourteen . . . I'd work for about six months to make the money to come back . . . to come back for the night life. I never lost contact with Ireland, even when I was touring the world." As if to prove the point, MacGowan's next album was to be his most Irish yet.

EIGHTEEN

The Return Of The Mac

Sightings of Shane MacGowan in the early part of 1997 were relatively few and far between. While he was occasionally spotted in pubs as far apart as Islington, Temple Fortune, Limerick and Cork, Shane more or less kept his own counsel until September, when he returned to the stage for two sold out gigs with The Popes at Dublin's Mean Fiddler club. In essence, these concerts acted as advertisements for Shane's forthcoming album, *The Crock Of Gold*, which was finally released in November, 1997. The disc took its name directly from James Stephen's famous Irish novel, a tale tracing one man's fantastical journey towards spiritual enlightenment and, quite possibly, beyond.

A writer after MacGowan's heart, Stephens rejected all attempts at placing intellectual constraints on his work, preferring instead to champion "emotion, heart and soul". To this end, he filled *The Crock Of Gold* with simple, yet striking images, the most notable being the constant intercession of sprites, spirits and mischievous leprechauns who offer "advice" and "occasional counsel" to the book's unlikely hero – sometimes sending him in the right direction, sometimes not. Shane was so taken by Stephen's plot device, he decided to paint these "apparitions" for the cover of his album, eventually handing in a strange montage of grinning spectres warming themselves before a flaming crock. "Yeah, I painted the album cover," he later recalled, "those are malicious fairies from hell."

A far more gentle proposition than *The Snake, The Crock of Gold* found MacGowan largely abandoning his temporary infatuation with rock'n'roll in favour of "a back to basics" approach. Therefore, the electric guitars and screaming solos that cranked up material such as 'That Woman's Got Me Drinking' and '. . . Church Of The Holy Spook' were now replaced by fiddles, whistles and wooden box-tops. Nonetheless, *The Crock Of Gold* was no simple retread of *Red Roses For Me* or *Rum, Sodomy And The Lash,* but more a rounding up of various Irish musical styles. "The album is my attempt at covering all aspects of Irish music," Shane confirmed. "People think there's only one type of Irish music, (but) this album takes you through the whole spectrum – Ceilidh, showband, punk, rock'n'roll, traditional . . . know what I mean?" As if to drive home the point, MacGowan was pictured on the back of the record sitting below a picture of legendary showband performer (and honorary citizen of Cricklewood), Big Tom.

Truthfully, *The Crock Of Gold* was partially compromised by the sheer weight of Shane's ambition, with the variety of styles on show never quite gelling into a workable whole. Though his backing band, The Popes, handled the transition from "electric overload to acoustic shimmer" admirably enough, the songs they had to work with were (with a few notable exceptions) not among MacGowan's best. In fact, tracks such as 'Céilidh Cowboy', 'Truck Drivin' Man' and the truly horrible cod-reggae of 'B&I Ferry' (actually co-written with the group) wouldn't have even made it onto a Pogues B-side from the years 1985 to 1989. Similarly, cover versions of the old traditional standards 'Spanish Lady' and 'Come To The Bower' sounded dull and lifeless, with Shane fighting to drag any emotion from them at all.

That said, when *The Crock Of Gold* did hit its stride, listeners had to fight hard to keep up. In 'Mother Mo Chroi' for instance, MacGowan had crafted another in a long line of fine "travellers' laments", this time drawing on his own personal experience of leaving Ireland as a young boy in 1962. "The day we sailed away, I remember it so well, I took one last look at the North Wall and bid a fond farewell." 'St. John Of Gods', too, pushed all the right buttons, its moving lyric telling of a man Shane encountered whilst drying out in a Dublin detox centre. "See the man . . . with the crushed up Carolls packet in his hand . . . all he says is 'F yez all, F yez all' . . ." The song was given added poignancy by the line, "Dragging him away from his crucified Lord," MacGowan's knowing reference to the real St. John of Gods, who took on the task of looking after Jesus' mother as he was nailed to the cross.

Two further tunes, 'More Pricks Than Kicks' and 'Lonesome Highway' provided strong evidence that Shane could still deliver the emotional goods when he chose to. With '. . . Kicks', the emphasis was firmly placed on self-flagellation, the singer seemingly admitting that in his rush to find the bar, life had all but passed him by. "I'm a scumbag, a lout . . . that's the way things are." Yet, on 'Lonesome Highway', he had recovered sufficiently to redirect his gaze towards the world, chronicling a variety of encounters with the lost and the loveless. "Livin' by night and hiding from the day . . ." Sadly, 'Lonesome Highway' failed to chart when released as a single in October, 1997.

In contrast to previous outings, *The Crock Of Gold* also demonstrated a new level of honesty in MacGowan's lyricism, especially in his dealing with matters of political correctness. For instance, the album's opening three tracks all carried the word "Paddy" in their title: 'Paddy Rolling Stone', 'Rock 'N' Roll Paddy' and most notoriously, 'Paddy Public Enemy No. 1'. "He shot a couple of coppers and he joined the IRA, and the papers called him 'Paddy Public Enemy No. 1'." Stirring up some controversy at the time, many thought the song to be about Dominic 'Mad Dog' McGlinchey, a former

IRA gunman and one time leader of the INLA. While Shane admitted McGlinchey's story provided the initial inspiration for '. . . No. 1', he was keen not to align himself directly with "the most wanted terrorist in Ireland". "It's about an IRA man," he offered at the time, "but no one in particular. It's just a story. I'm *not* expressing an opinion about the IRA." Yet, critics persisted, pointing to the lyrics of another . . . *Crock Of Gold* tune, 'Skipping Rhymes': "We put the hood around his head, then we shot the bastard dead . . . with a nick nack paddy wack, give a dog a bone, send the stupid bastards home."

Again, MacGowan defended himself eloquently, pointing to the fact that he didn't write the lyrics or the tune, but simply heard it being sung by children in the street. "It's just children's street rhymes which I heard them singing." He told the *Irish Post*'s Jim Conlon. "It sends chills down your spine, but I suppose they don't know anything else really." In truth, castigating Shane for including the likes of 'Paddy Public Enemy No. 1' and 'Skipping Rhymes' on *The Crock Of Gold* was a largely redundant exercise. After all, his stated intention with the album was to capture Ireland's spirit and, like it or not, rebel songs were an intrinsic part of the country's musical heritage. Besides, MacGowan was wholly behind the peace process in Northern Ireland, even going as far as to champion the efforts of political leaders such as Gerry Adams. "The Irish struggle is about freedom and slavery," he stated, "and Gerry Adams is a man who can do it . . . (bring about peace). He's a massive intelligence and has a lack of bitterness about crying over spilt milk. I don't think he was born for crucifixion. I think he was born for a kingdom . . . he's a high king, the man who will unite a nation."

Produced solely by MacGowan, *The Crock Of Gold* came to a jarring halt at number 59 in the UK album charts on November 8, 1997. One week later, the album had disappeared altogether, a victim of poor promotion, public disinterest and some decidedly mixed reviews: "The dentally challenged boozy Irish bard's slurry tales of drinking, high times and the IRA finally become fiddle-dee-dee by numbers," said *Q*'s Anthony Thornton, "and now even his lyrics fail to ignite the emotions the way he once could do so effortlessly." *Mojo*'s Neil Spencer was even more terse in his assessment of Shane's latest offering. "You know you're in trouble – or rather Shane MacGowan is – when you're confronted with titles like 'Lonesome Highway' and 'Truck Drivin' Man'," Spencer stated, "these days (he) is principally a master of cliché . . . a reminder that the pint-pot muse is a particularly fickle mistress."

There were, however, a few supporters left, including *Vox*'s Gavin Martin: "The prodigal son of the post-punk, folk-fucking, rowdy romantic rebel shtick . . . continues to defy all reasonable expectations for his artistic, let alone life expectancy. Dropping into the world one Christmas morning nearly 40 years ago, Shane has always bounced back from invariably self-inflicted obstacles to assert his superiority over whatever gym-friendly, Perrier-supping shitehawks may be standing in his wake . . . and the best music on *The Crock Of Gold* will be around long after those comments about not looking too healthy have joined similarly redundant observations about the Pope's religious persuasion and the bear's toilet habits. (*The Crock Of Gold*) is savagely beautiful." Unsurprisingly, MacGowan agreed: "It's the best album I've done since *If I Should Fall From Grace With God*. I wanted to get right back to the roots . . . back to pure Irish music, simple songs with lots of humour, emotion, energy and anger."

Whatever its strengths or weaknesses, *The Crock Of Gold* still performed badly "at the box office", leaving Shane in the unenviable position of touring on the back of a record few had heard, let alone bought. Fortunately, the media once again rallied around him, this time in the form of the BBC, who broadcast a documentary about the singer's life in the spring of 1998. Taking its name from an affecting phrase used to describe the Irish potato famine of 1845–50 (in which countless thousands died), *The Great Hunger* presented a reasonably sympathetic portrait of Shane, covering his childhood in Tipperary, decade with The Pogues and subsequent solo career. Much attention was also given to MacGowan's contribution to Irish folk music and culture, with celebrities such as U2's Bono, Nick Cave and Sinéad O'Connor all lining up to endorse his achievements, if not his lifestyle. "He's operating on two engines (instead) of four," Sinéad offered of her wayward friend. "He's a genius when he's completely fucked up. Imagine how much more of a genius he'd be if he wasn't. I hope he doesn't smash himself entirely, because it's an incredible beauty that he has." Fellow musician Christy Moore kept his comments brief, but wholly to the point: "Bejesus, you know how to write them, boy, I'll tell you."

The programme ended with The Dubliners' Ronnie Drew performing a poignant a cappella version of 'The Dunes' – a song Shane had written to commemorate those who perished in the famine of the 1840s. "As we died in vain, they stole our grain to put upon their tables, the dying covered the dead with sand and danced while they were able." Contrasting MacGowan's photo-realistic imagery against eye-witness accounts gathered at the time, it was sometimes difficult to believe he had written the tune some one hundred and fifty years after events unfolded. "Neither pen nor pencil could ever portray the misery and horror," wrote Irish artist James Mahony following a visit to Cork's Skibbereen district in 1847. ". . . I saw the dying, the living and the dead, lying indiscriminately upon the same floor, without anything between them and the cold earth, save a few miserable rags upon them."

Though *The Great Hunger* did little harm to Shane's reputation (it may well have even enhanced it), he remained irritated by some of the programme's editorial content. For instance, the production team was keen to draw attention to MacGowan's interest in the 19th century Republican poet, James Mangan –

perhaps for the purpose of establishing parallels between the two men – who after all – did share a similar love of both Ireland and alcohol. Yet, Shane felt Mangan's presence throughout the documentary was disproportionate in comparison to his other literary influences, which included writers such as James Stephens, Flann O'Brian, Brendan Behan and the renowned Spanish bard, Lorca. "It's just their view, you know what I mean?" he later said. Apparently, the singer was also annoyed that both his family and long-standing girlfriend, Victoria Clarke, were interviewed on camera. "I can't understand why anyone would be that interested," MacGowan reasoned. As ever though, he remained brutally honest when asked why he agreed to participate in the first place. "Money . . . but I didn't enjoy it much."

Despite his misgivings, Shane MacGowan had benefited from being given "the serious treatment" by the BBC. Long overdue, *The Great Hunger* granted him a life beyond "the drunken Paddy angle" and reacquainted fans, past and present, with the true nature of his gift. To wit: "great stories and great songs, well told and well sung." As if to emphasise the point, Shane once again took to the road for a surprisingly virile string of concert dates throughout 1998. Though personal mobility was not at a premium (he had broken his hip the year before, allegedly falling from a bar stool), MacGowan nevertheless appeared at Dublin's Point Depot on March 17, before taking on a short European tour in the late spring. By June, he was back in England, performing at Fleadh '98 alongside such well-established acts as Sinéad O'Connor, Dr. John, The Waterboys' Mike Scott and an up and coming Irish band named The Corrs, who in a remarkably short space of time would come to represent the new face of Nineties Ireland – a face, incidentally, politicians and businessmen were keen to promote, and which The Pogues had inadvertently done so much to undermine.

The summer of 1998 brought more MacGowan related

activity, though this time it was Shane's younger sister, Siobhan, who found herself in the spotlight. A fine singer/ songwriter, Siobhan's recently released album, *Chariot*, had garnered impressive reviews from all corners of the music press, with one critic describing her as a cross between "Patsy Cline and The Velvet Underground". If one also included Van Morrison circa *Astral Weeks*, *Bryter Layter* period Nick Drake and a liberal smattering of Mazzy Star, then *Chariot*'s rich, evocative sound began to make sense. While Siobhan's approach to the business of making music was far more contemporary than that of her elder brother, she still shared his penchant for writing timeless melodies, with songs such as 'Trust Me', 'Well-Worn Smile' and the engaging 'Celtic Lullaby' stretching across the decades in thoroughly agreeable fashion.

A creative dynasty now in the offing, Shane MacGowan again withdrew from public duties to concentrate on the important things in life – writing songs, drinking at his favourite North London pub and watching Clint Eastwood and Sam Peckinpah videos. However, over the next two years, his patience would be tested by a series of well-meaning, if largely futile interventions, several senseless deaths and the unerring gaze of the popular press. If, as so many seemed to believe, MacGowan was truly invulnerable, then now would be the time to prove it.

NINETEEN

They Call You Lady Luck . . .

"They call you Lady Luck, but there is room for doubt.
At times you have a very unlady-like way of running
  out . . ."

                     – 'Luck Be A Lady'

For the majority of 1999, Shane MacGowan's life continued apace. A short tour here, a few drinks there. No major changes, just business as usual. There were rumours that another solo album, the engagingly titled *20th Century Paddy*, would hit the shops before the year was out and Shane seemed genuinely enthusiastic about its contents. "It's going to be a double album, yeah?" he told the *Irish Voice*'s Tom Dunphy. "One (disc) is going to be old numbers like 'Carrickfergus' and 'Spancil Hill'. Then there's broken-hearted love ballads. A Carolans-type instrumental called 'Victoria Clarke', some O'Riada style music . . . and a blasting Paddy-beat the whole way through . . ."

Things had evidently changed since 1998, when MacGowan promised his next LP would contain the word "Paddy" in every song title – a sly way, according to the singer, of rescuing the term from its negative historical connotations and giving it the true majesty it deserved. Sadly, *20th Century Paddy* failed to materialise, its stalled release allegedly due to behind-the-

187

scenes problems MacGowan encountered with his record company, ZTT. This souring of relations began as early as 1997 when ZTT encountered problems in promoting *The Crock Of Gold* in the USA. "There were some very controversial lyrics in there," drummer Danny Pope later confirmed. "There was feedback from America, where they didn't like the lyrics on one or two tracks."

For Shane, it was the latest development in a love/hate relationship with the States that had lasted the best part of two decades. In his early days with The Pogues, he was often vocally supportive of the country, even making noises about living there one day. "Make yourself a bit of dough," MacGowan said in 1984, "get a few guns to protect yourself and you're all right." Yet, years of touring gradually wore down his enthusiasm, with Shane growing ever more tired of endless highways, cramped tour buses and monochrome hotel rooms. By 1999, a partial truce between Shane and America had been established, though he still blew hot and cold when the occasion warranted it. "I like the people," MacGowan said of Boston, following his performance at Guinness Fleadh '99, "but there's nothing happening (here). It's not open all night . . . not like New York." Sensing a breakdown in international relations, Joey Cashman soon came to Shane's rescue: "He gets an idea in his head," Cashman told *Amplifier*'s Elaine McArdle. "He has a good time in a bar and then he determines a city is brilliant."

MacGowan's personal manager since his exit from The Pogues in 1991, Joey Cashman, had grown well used to smoothing over the various cracks opened by his unpredictable charge. A member of The Pogues' inner sanctum since the mid-Eighties (when he pulled double duty as a tenor sax player on *If I Should Fall From Grace With God* and *Peace And Love*, as well as handling the band's insane touring schedule), Cashman was responsible for all aspects of Shane's career, from personal finances to recording commitments. Respected as much for his business acumen as his ability to keep MacGowan in sight of the "straight and narrow", Cashman must have been overjoyed with the series of events set in motion by Sinéad O'Connor in November, 1999.

A close friend of Shane's for some years, Sinéad had visited the singer in his North London flat only to find him allegedly snorting heroin. Following a terse exchange of views on the subject of drugs, O'Connor left MacGowan to his own devices. However, conscience soon compelled her to notify the police of his behaviour. "I love Shane," she said after the incident, "but it makes me angry to see him destroy himself selfishly in front of those who love him." She continued: "I reported him to the police for his own good. I never wanted him put in prison because drugs are freely available there, but ordered into a rehabilitation programme."

MacGowan, however, was having none of it. "I might as well clear up the fact that she's made out I was lying on the floor in a coma," he told the *Observer*'s Andrew Anthony, "whereas in fact, I was sitting on the sofa having a G&T, watching a Sam Peckinpah movie, *Cross Of Iron*." By the time he appeared as a guest on Irish TV's *The Late Late Show*, Shane was openly accusing Sinéad of "shopping him for publicity purposes".

Whatever the truth of the matter, The Crown Prosecution Service declined to act on O'Connor's accusations, despite the fact that MacGowan admitted to possession of heroin at the time of the incident. It was a shabby end to a genuine friendship, with both sides soon directing all enquiries regarding the story through their managers, the possibility of legal reprisal following their war of words outweighing the need to clarify any loose ends. However, Sinéad's very public airing of Shane's dirty laundry led to other, more gruesome stories resurfacing – specifically the high proliferation of drug and alcohol related deaths surrounding MacGowan and The Popes since 1995.

In truth, Shane was no stranger to mortality. Aside from the loss of various relations, the singer had seen one of his best friends, Pogues lighting man Paul Verner, die from alcohol related illness in 1993. "Awful." He said at the time. "Brandy is poison. The worst. A killer." By 1997, another of MacGowan's close associates, Charlie Maclennan, passed away – though this time Shane was able to capture his spirit in song, with Maclennan providing the lead vocal on a tremulous version of Lerner and Loewe's 1969 hit 'Wand'rin' Star' (the track subsequently appeared on *The Crock Of Gold*). Still, it was the untimely demises of Dave Jordan, Brian Ging and Robbie O'Neil that really drew the attention of the press to MacGowan's door. In a comprehensive article in Ireland's *Sunday Independent*, journalist Michael Sheridan pointed to the fact that Jordan, Ging and O'Neil were all "in Shane's orbit" when they succumbed to fatal overdoses, with O'Neil actually expiring at the singer's North London home on May 17, 1999.

Though Sheridan drew the line at suggesting MacGowan had provided them with drugs (or indeed encouraged their experimentation), he nevertheless made it clear that these young men may have been unduly influenced by the hedonistic atmosphere surrounding the ex-Pogue. "What makes me angry," said one of the (unnamed) contributors to Sheridan's article, "is that the culture was established and spread to other people. No one forced them to take the drug, but the fact is three of my best friends – working for the band in one way or another – are now dead. That makes me very bitter and sad, but Shane doesn't seem to have taken on board (the fact that) he could be next." In MacGowan's defence, Sheridan noted that all three men had prominent ties with the music industry – a business renowned for turning a blind eye to both alcohol and narcotics abuse. In fact, both Jordan and O'Neil were professional sound engineers, whilst Ging was a prominent "face about town", often to be found attending various concerts and shows in the London area. Equally as important, each man had a previous history of drug use – though only

Jordan was known to be addicted to heroin at the time of his demise.

Indeed, Shane responded to all of Michael Sheridan's enquiries, making it clear that while he deeply regretted the death of his three friends, he felt no responsibility for their actions. "I don't want heroin in my place," MacGowan said. "My place is my place, and I don't want any of that shit in my house." He continued. "It's all too depressing . . . all these people . . . and I don't want to discuss it. But most of the people that worked with The Pogues and The Popes are all still alive – *I'm still alive* – and I think I'm in good shape." Perhaps. Or perhaps not. As ever, Shane's continued well-being was of grave concern to those around him – so much so in fact, that he was finally admitted to the world famous Priory clinic in February, 2000. A medical institution renowned for helping celebrities overcome drink/drug addictions, The Priory's previous guests included the likes of Robbie Williams and Kate Moss. Discreetly hidden from public view by iron gates, stone walls and a towering array of oak trees, the Roehampton retreat was seen as a veritable 'Mecca' to those pop stars, actors and supermodels rich enough to gain access to its leafy grounds.

Not so MacGowan. Within two weeks of entry, the singer was ejected from the premises for continuing bouts of "unreasonable behaviour". "The Priory?" he later growled. "It had a love cross outside and was full of priests. They were all buggering each other . . ." Obviously mortified by what he found there, Shane put as much distance as possible between him and the clinic by booking a quick tour of the USA, which included dates in New York and Boston's Harp Club. However, on September 25, 2000, he returned to the scene of his previous crimes, voluntarily checking himself in for a protracted stay at The Priory's other site in Southgate, North London. On this occasion, MacGowan lasted a princely twenty-four hours before signing out once again. Keen to establish the elasticity of his intentions, he was back in Southgate by October 9, but as with previous visits, chose to leave within a day or so. Suffice it to say, several further efforts to "get with the programme" all ended without success.

Evidently, MacGowan's desire for change was superseded by 'the habit of a lifetime', his love affair with drink too precious a thing to abandon for the sake of sobriety. However, the sheer number of visits Shane made to The Priory in 2000 suggest he may at last be facing up to the fact he has a problem. While some may laugh at the obviousness of such a statement, MacGowan has always denied alcoholism, preferring instead to consider himself "an addictive personality". "I drink to relax," he once said. "I am a slow drinker, not a desperate drinker." Yet, there is an old Irish saying he may be all too familiar with: "First the man takes a drink. Then the drink takes a drink. Then, the drink takes the man . . ." Where Shane sits on the scale is ultimately a question only he can answer.

TWENTY

The Measure Of A Man

February 2001

The years on either side of the Millennium were not easy for Shane MacGowan. Since his public falling out with Sinéad O'Connor in November, 1999, the songwriter found himself the source of continued media attention, his various comings and goings at The Priory, The Met Bar – or indeed any bar – providing valuable column inches for the tabloid press. Given his various proclivities, and unfailing honesty when a microphone is thrust towards him, one might argue that Shane encourages such speculation – a life writ large as his own proving too tasty a treat for journalists to ignore. Yet, beyond the grainy images of MacGowan emerging from rehabilitation, or more likely a certain Islington pub, he continues to talk of music and the inevitable release of his third solo album, *20th Century Paddy*. "It's about IRA men and lonely farmers who hang themselves because they can't get a wife." Following his break with ZTT, the title may well have to change to accommodate the new Millennium.

Of course, he continues to tour, with the UK, USA and Europe providing lucrative stomping grounds for both himself and The Popes. However, recent years have seen his backing band occasionally strike out on their own. "Because Shane doesn't do (as many concerts), it would mean we'd do a couple of gigs with him and get fairly tight . . . and then we'd all disappear." John 'The Riddler' Myers told *Rock 'n' Reel*'s Nick Moulton, "The buzz would go away and we'd have to start again. But when we started doing our own thing, it kept us all fairly tight and in touch with one another."

In fact, the policy proved so successful that The Popes have already released their first album, *Holloway Boulevard*, on Snapper Records. Aside from several original compositions, as well as a number of traditional melodies, the group have covered three brand new MacGowan originals, including 'Chino's Place' and the bracing 'Pump Action Paddy'. Over in nostalgia corner, Spider Stacy, Andrew Ranken and Daryll Hunt all returned from relative obscurity in the early months of 1999 to perform a string of concert dates under the guise of The Wisemen. Sadly, the reunion proved brief, with the ex-Pogues seemingly content to disappear once again into the musical ether. Like his former colleagues, Jem Finer also resurfaced in 1999 as part of the new act Longplayer. But as with The Wisemen, little has been heard or seen from them in the last year or so.

On a much more tragic note, long-time Pogues associate Kirsty MacColl was killed on December 20, 2000, the forty-one-year-old singer struck by a speedboat while swimming off a beach in Mexico. "She was the perfect girl to sing 'Fairytale Of New York'." MacGowan confirmed soon after hearing of the MacColl's demise. "She was always brilliant, an amazing woman – funny and intelligent. Kirsty had a lot of demons in her life, but she never put it on to others. She was always up and raring to go . . . enjoying life." In a strange twist of fate, MacColl had actually spoken of death just before the release of her final record, the Latin-tinged *Tropical Brainstorm*. "Whenever I go into the studio," she said, "I always operate on the principle that I might get hit by a bus tomorrow. And I would hate the obituaries to read, 'Her last album was her not very good album.'" Thankfully, the album in question was one of her very best.

And so to the man himself.

As ever, Shane MacGowan's future remains uncertain. In all honesty, it has done for the last decade or so, with numerous editorials, articles and essays predicting "an early bath" for the hard-living Irishman. MacGowan for one, is heartily sick of such attention, forever pointing to the fact that he is very much in the land of the living. "The drink and the drugs make for a neat little . . . story." He has said, "The media are always looking for someone to put into that particular box – Keith Richards, Iggy Pop, myself – and I might have slept in it for a while, but I managed to crawl out of the fucker." His girl-friend, Victoria Clarke, also dismisses talk of Shane's so-called death wish, giving stark testimony to the opposite point of view. "He has a genuine will to live," Clarke told the BBC in 1998, "a genuine will to be alive. Yet, it doesn't appear that way. People think he must have a death wish, but in actual fact, that's not the case. He just doesn't enjoy life without a drink . . ."

The drink. Belfast writer Garth Ennis calls it "Irish inevitabil-ity" – a curse (or blessing) so ingrained in the culture and its people that it would take a book in itself to analyse its effects. Suffice it to say, the Irish are as much associated with drink as they are with gallows humour, romantic whimsy and unswerv-ing hospitality. Perceptions are changing, however. The latest crop of pop exports to escape the Emerald Isle appear to have been brought up on nothing more ruinous than spring water and rice cakes, the likes of The Corrs, Boyzone, Bewitched and Westlife all glowing with health – their eyes button-bright, their bank balances overflowing as a result. Of course, there is nothing wrong with a life well lived. After all, temperance, they tell us, is a virtue leading to sainthood. And Ireland knows all about saints. Yet, in the face of such seeming perfection, MacGowan's ongoing battle to encourage his country to accept its roots and revel in its musical traditions appears lost, or at least severely compromised.

In reality, Shane may well be the last of a dying breed, the product of a thousand late night lock-ins where poitín is served in dirty glasses and no one gives a damn. Certainly, since the release of 1997's *The Crock Of Gold,* he has run the danger of slipping into cultural myth, a man as renowned for his lifestyle as his way with a tune. One can only witness the evidence. *Viz* magazine's painfully funny comic strip *The Adventures Of Little Shane MacGowan* and, more recently, *Is Shane MacGowan Still Alive?,* a book whose title manages to both lionise and lampoon him in equal measure. At times, he must wonder whether it's all been worth it.

The answer must be yes. Despite Shane's failings, his body of work remains largely unequalled in recent Irish traditional folk, or indeed, most pop – the sheer depth of lyrical and melodic invention a source of constant wonder to critics and fans alike. With compositions such as 'The Old Main Drag', 'If I Should Fall From Grace With God', 'A Rainy Night In Soho' and the immortal 'Fairytale Of New York', MacGowan rewrote many of the rules of "the Celtic standard", dragging the music through images of contemporary urban decay, drug addiction and prostitution, yet without losing an ounce of its romanticism or power along the way. For that fact alone, he deserves commendation.

Of course, following Shane's progress has been an infuriating business at times. The lapses in concentration, the resolutely anti-intellectual stance and the continuing threat of alcohol or drugs ruining it all for good have often acted as barriers to his cause, distancing those who might otherwise proclaim his talent, and testing the patience of those already on his side. Nonetheless, the sheer honesty of MacGowan's attitude continues to beguile, the wry self-knowledge he exercises in everyday life outweighing his various faults and foibles. "I've had a very happy life," he confirmed. "If they stuck me in a box tomorrow, I'd know I'd had a bloody whale of a time. How many people have made loads of money, done every drug under the rising sun, gone out every night and been around the world before they're thirty? A few maybe, but I'm one of the *lucky* few."

What Shane MacGowan has done with his life, he has obviously done out of choice. Finding his road early, he stubbornly defies revival, rehabilitation, or indeed, any other attempt to aid or alter his course. Whether that makes him a madman or a genius depends on your point of view. Yet, it's unlikely to affect him either way. "I have suffered, because life is suffering," MacGowan once said. "But it's also a fucking pleasure. You can't separate the two. It's partly knowing that it's not going to last that makes happiness so wonderful. It will be struck down in the end, so you got to grab it while you can. That's the thing everyone misses. I'm just following the Irish tradition of songwriting – the Irish way of life, the human way of life. Cram as much pleasure as you can into life, and then rail against the pain you suffer as a result." In typical fashion, he even knows what he wants written on his tombstone. "Fuck you! It's an attitude I've been faithful to . . ."

No argument there.

DISCOGRAPHY

7″ & 12″ Singles, EPs and CDs
(All UK releases unless otherwise stated)

The Nipple Erectors

King Of The Bop/Nervous Wreck
Soho SH 1/2 7″ June 1978 (Limited edition single – 50 copies pressed)

The Nips

All The Time In The World/Private Eyes
Soho SH 4 7″ August 1979

Gabrielle/Vengeance
Soho SH 9 7″ February 1980

Gabrielle/Vengeance
Soho SH 9 7″ 1980 (Picture sleeve, with 'Licensed To Cool' stamp on cover. Limited to 100 copies)

Gabrielle/Vengeance
Chiswick CHIS 119 7″ May 1980 (Re-issue)

Happy Song/Nobody To Love
Test Pressing TP 5 7″ October 1981

Pogue Mahone

Dark Streets of London/The Band Played Waltzing Matilda
Pogue Mahone PM-1 7″ May 1984

Dark Streets Of London/The Band Played Waltzing Matilda
Pogue Mahone PM-1 7″ May 1984 (White label/picture sleeve
featuring 'Harp' illustration – limited edition, only 237 copies
issued)

The Pogues

Dark Streets Of London/The Band Played Waltzing Matilda
Stiff BUY 207 7″ June 1984

Boys From The County Hell/Repeal Of The Licensing Laws
Stiff BUY 212 7″ October 1984

Dark Streets Of London/The Band Played Waltzing Matilda/
Boys From The County Hell/Repeal Of The Licensing Laws
Stiff BUY 207/212 7″ November 1984 (Limited edition
double-pack single)

A Pair Of Brown Eyes/Whiskey You're The Devil
Stiff Buy 220 7″ March 1985

A Pair Of Brown Eyes/Whiskey You're The Devil
Stiff Buy 220 7″ March 1985 (Picture disc)

A Pair Of Brown Eyes/Whiskey You're The Devil/Muirshin
Durkin
Stiff BUYIT 220 12″ March 1985

Boys From The County Hell/Repeal Of The Licensing Laws/
A Pair Of Brown Eyes/Whiskey You're The Devil
Stiff BUY 212/220 7″ March 1985 (Limited edition double-pack
single)

Sally MacLennane/Wild Rover
Stiff BUY 224 7″ June 1985

Sally MacLennane/Wild Rover
Stiff BUY 224 7″ June 1985 (Green vinyl edition with poster)

Sally MacLennane/Wild Rover
Stiff PBUY 224 7″ June 1985 (Picture disc)

Sally MacLennane/Wild Rover/The Leaving Of Liverpool
Stiff BUYIT 224 12″ June 1985

Sally MacLennane/Wild Rover/The Leaving Of Liverpool/
The Wild Cats Of Kilkenny
Stiff BUYC 224 (Cassette) June 1985

Dirty Old Town/A Pistol For Paddy Garcia
Stiff BUY 229 7″ August 1985

Dirty Old Town/A Pistol For Paddy Garcia
Stiff PBUY 229 7″ August 1985 (Picture disc)

Dirty Old Town/A Pistol For Paddy Garcia/The Parting Glass
Stiff BUYIT 229 12″ August 1985

Dirty Old Town (Live)/Sally MacLennane (Live)/Band Interview
Stiff MAIL 3 12″ August 1985 (Mail order only)

Poguetry In Motion (EP)
A Rainy Night In Soho/The Body Of An American/London Girl/
Planxty Noel Hill
Stiff BUY 243 EP February 1986

Poguetry In Motion (EP)
A Rainy Night In Soho/The Body Of An American/London Girl/
Planxty Noel Hill
Stiff PBUY 243 EP February 1986 (Picture disc)

Poguetry In Motion (EP)
A Rainy Night In Soho/The Body Of An American/London
Girl/Planxty Noel Hill
Stiff BUYIT 243 12″ EP February 1986

Haunted/Junk Theme
MCA 1084 7″ August 1986

Haunted/Junk Theme/Hot Dogs With Everything
MCA MCAT 1084 12″ August 1986

The Good, The Bad And The Ugly/Rake At The Gates Of Hell
Stiff HELL BLOOD 1 7″ 1987 (Unreleased)

The Good, The Bad And The Ugly/Rake At The Gates Of Hell
Stiff HELL BLOODY 1 12″ 1987 (Unreleased)

St. Patrick's Night (EP)
A Pair Of Brown Eyes (Live)/Dirty Old Town (Live)
Pogue Mahone SGG 1–12 12″ February 1988

If I Should Fall From Grace With God/Sally MacLennane (Live)
Pogue Mahone FG 1 7″ February 1988

If I Should Fall From Grace With God/Sally MacLennane (Live)/
A Pair Of Brown Eyes (Live)/Dirty Old Town (Live)
Pogue Mahone FG 12 12″ February 1988

Fiesta/Sketches Of Spain
Pogue Mahone FG 2 7″ July 1988

Fiesta/Sketches Of Spain/South Australia
Pogue Mahone FG 12 12″ July 1988

Yeah, Yeah, Yeah, Yeah, Yeah/Limerick Rake
WEA YZ 355 7″ December 1988

Yeah, Yeah, Yeah, Yeah, Yeah/Limerick Rake/Honky Tonk Women
WEA YZ 355 12 12″ December 1988

Yeah, Yeah, Yeah, Yeah, Yeah (Edit)/Limerick Rake/Yeah, Yeah,
Yeah, Yeah, Yeah (Long Version)/Honky Tonk Women
WEA YZ 355 CD CD December 1988

Misty Morning, Albert Bridge/Cotton Fields
WEA YZ 407 7″ June 1989

Misty Morning, Albert Bridge/Cotton Fields/Young Ned Of The
Hill/Train Of Love
WEA YZ 407 T 12 12″ June 1989

Misty Morning, Albert Bridge/Misty Morning, Albert Bridge
WEA SAM 553 12″ June 1989 (Green Vinyl Promotional Release)

Misty Morning, Albert Bridge/Cotton Fields/Young Ned Of The
Hill/Train Of Love
WEA YZ 407 CD CD June 1989

White City/Every Man Is A King
WEA YZ 409 7" August 1989

White City/Maggie May (Live)/Every Man Is A King
WEA YZ 409 TX 12" August 1989

White City/Every Man Is A King/The Star Of The County Down
WEA YZ 409 CD CD August 1989

Summer In Siam/Bastard Landlord
WEA YZ 519 7" August 1990

Summer In Siam/Bastard Landlord/Hell's Ditch (Instrumental)
WEA YZ 519 T 12" August 1990

Summer In Siam/Bastard Landlord/Hell's Ditch (Instrumental)/
The Irish Rover
WEA YZ 519 CD CD August 1990

Sayonara/Curse Of Love/Infinity
WEA CD (Catalogue number unavailable) April 1991

A Rainy Night In Soho(Remix)/Squid Out Of Water
WEA YZ 603 7" September 1991

A Rainy Night In Soho/Squid Out Of Water/Infinity
WEA YZ 603 T September 1991

A Rainy Night In Soho/Squid Out Of Water/Infinity
WEA YZ 603 CD CD September 1991

Honky Tonk Women/Curse Of Love
WEA YZ 673 7" May 1992

Honky Tonk Women/Curse Of Love/Infinity
WEA YZ 673 T 12" May 1992

Honky Tonk Women/Curse Of Love/Infinity/The Parting Glass
WEA YZ 673 CD CD May 1992

Tuesday Morning/First Day Of Forever
WEA YZ 758 7" August 1993

Tuesday Morning/First Day Of Forever/Turkish Song Of The
Damned (Live)
WEA YZ 758 CD CD August 1993

Tuesday Morning/London Calling (Live)/I Fought The Law (Live)
WEA YZ 758 CDX CD August 1993

Once Upon A Time/Train Kept Rolling On
WEA YZ 777 7" January 1994

Once Upon A Time/Train Kept Rolling On/Tuesday Morning/
Paris St. Germain
WEA YZ 777 C CD January 1994

How Come/Eyes Of An Angel
WEA 011 X 7" September 1995

How Come/Eyes Of An Angel/Tuesday Morning (Live)/Big City
(Live)
WEA WX 011 CD CD September 1995

The Pogues Featuring Kirsty MacColl

Fairytale Of New York/The Battle March Medley
Pogue Mahone NY 7 7" November 1987

Fairytale Of New York/The Battle March Medley/Shane Bradley
Pogue Mahone NY 12 12" November 1987

Fairytale Of New York/The Battle March Medley/Shane Bradley
Pogue Mahone CDNY 1 CD November 1987

Fairytale Of New York/Fiesta
WEA YZ 628 7" December 1991

Fairytale Of New York/Fiesta/A Pair Of Brown Eyes/
Sick Bed Of Cúchulainn/Maggie May
WEA YZ 628 T 12" December 1991

Fairytale Of New York/Fiesta/A Pair Of Brown Eyes/
Sick Bed Of Cúchulainn/Maggie May
WEA YZ 628 CD CD December 1991

Miss Otis Regrets/Just One Of Those Things
Chrysalis 7" November 1990 (Catalogue number unavailable)

The Pogues & The Dubliners

The Irish Rover/The Rare Old Mountain Dew
Stiff BUY 258 7" March 1987

The Irish Rover/The Rare Old Mountain Dew/The Dubliner's
Fancy
Stiff BUY 258 IT 12" March 1987

Jack's Heroes/Whiskey In The Jar
WEA YZ 500 7" May 1990

Jack's Heroes/Whiskey In The Jar/Long Version
WEA YZ 500 T 12" May 1990

Jack's Heroes/Whiskey In The Jar/Long Version
WEA YZ 500 CD CD May 1990

Albums
(All UK CD releases unless otherwise stated)

The Nips

Only Happy At The Beginning
I Love To Make You Cry/Vengeance/Gabrielle/King Of The
Bop/Ghost Town/Fuss 'N' Bother/Venus In Bovver
Boots/Happy Song/Stupid Cow/Nobody To
Love/Infatuation/Maida Aida/Hit Parade/Can't Say No
Soho HOHO 1 LP October 1980

Bops, Babes, Booze & Bovver
King Of The Bop/Nervous Wreck/So Pissed Off/Stavordale Rd.
N5/All The Time In The World/Private Eye/Gabrielle/
Vengeance
Big Beat WIKM 66 LP December 1987

The Pogues

Red Roses For Me
Transmetropolitan/The Battle Of Brisbane/The Auld Triangle/
Waxie's Gargle/Boys From The County Hell/Sea Shanty/
Dark Streets Of London/Streams Of Whiskey/Poor Paddy/
Dingle Regatta/Greenland Whale Fisheries/Down In The
Ground Where The Dead Men Go/Kitty
Stiff SEEZ 55 LP September 1984
WEA 2292 44492 2 CD re-issue January 1989

Rum, Sodomy And The Lash
The Sick Bed Of Cúchulainn/The Old Main Drag/Wild Cats Of
Kilkenny/I'm A Man You Don't Meet Every Day/A Pair Of Brown
Eyes/Sally MacLennane/Dirty Old Town/Jesse James/
Navigator/Billy's Bones/The Gentleman Soldier/And The Band
Played Waltzing Matilda
Stiff SEEZ 58 LP August 1985
WEA 2292 44495 2 CD re-issue January 1989
(Contains one bonus track – 'A Pistol For Paddy Garcia')

If I Should Fall From Grace With God
If I Should Fall From Grace With God/Turkish Song Of The
Damned/Bottle Of Smoke/Fairytale Of New York/Metropolis/
Thousands Are Sailing/Medley: The Recruiting Sergeant – The
Rocky Road To Dublin – Galway Races/Streets Of Sorrow –
Birmingham Six/Lullaby Of London/Sit Down By The Fire/
The Broad Majestic Shannon/Worms
Pogue Mahone NYR 1 90872 LP January 1988
WEA 2292 44493 2 CD re-issue January 1989
(Contains two bonus tracks – South Australia and The Battle
March Medley)

Peace And Love
Gridlock/White City/Young Ned Of The Hill/Misty Morning,
Albert Bridge/Cotton Fields/Blue Heaven/Down All The Days/
USA/Lorelei/Gartloney Rats/Boat Train/Tombstone/
Night Train To Lorca/London You're A Lady
WEA WX 2292 46086 2 247 91225 LP July 1989
WEA 2292 46086 2 CD July 1989

Hell's Ditch
The Sunnyside Of The Street/Sayonara/The Ghost Of A Smile/
Hell's Ditch/Lorca's Novena/Summer In Siam/Rain Street/
Rainbow Man/The Wake Of The Medusa/House Of The Gods/
5 Green Queens And Jean/Maidrin Rua/Six To Go
WEA WX 9031 725554 2 366 422846 LP September 1990
WEA 9031 725554 2 CD September 1990

Waiting For Herb
Tuesday Morning/Smell Of Petroleum/Haunting/Once Upon A
Time/Sitting On Top Of The World/Drunken Boat/Big City/
Girl From The Wadi Hammamat/Modern World/Pachinko/
My Baby's Gone/Small Hours
WEA WX 4509 93463 2 61598 LP September 1993
WEA 4509 93463 2 CD September 1993

Pogue Mahone
How Come/Living In A World Without Her/When The Ship
Comes In/Anniversary/Amadie/Love You Till The End/
Bright Lights/Oretown/Pont Mirabeau/Tosspint/Four O'clock
In The Morning/Where That Love's Been Gone/The Sun And
The Moon
WEA 0630 11210 241 LP October 1995
WEA 0630 11210 2 CD October 1995

Compilations/Collections:
(All UK releases unless otherwise stated)

The Pogues

The Best Of The Pogues
Fairytale Of New York/Sally MacLennane/Dirty Old Town/
The Irish Rover/A Pair Of Brown Eyes/Streams Of Whiskey/
A Rainy Night In Soho/Fiesta/Rain Street/Misty Morning, Albert
Bridge/White City/Thousands Are Sailing/The Broad Majestic
Shannon/The Body Of An American
WEA WX 9031 75405 2 430 September 1991
WEA 9031 75405 2 CD September 1991

The Rest Of The Best
If I Should Fall From Grace With God/The Sick Bed Of
Cúchulainn/The Old Main Drag/Boys From The County Hell/
Young Ned Of The Hill/Dark Streets Of London/
The Auld Triangle/Repeal Of The Licensing Laws/
Yeah, Yeah, Yeah, Yeah, Yeah/London Girl/Honky Tonk Women/
Summer In Siam/Turkish Song Of The Damned/
Lullaby Of London/The Sunnyside Of The Street/Hell's Ditch
WEA WX 9031 77341 2 471 June 1992
WEA 9031 77341 2 CD June 1992

Shane MacGowan & The Popes

Singles
(All UK releases unless otherwise stated)

The Church Of The Holy Spook/Rake At The Gates Of Hell
ZTT Zang 57 7" September 1994

The Church Of The Holy Spook/Rake At The Gates Of Hell/
King Of The Bop/Nancy Whisky
ZTT Zang 57 CDX CD September 1994
(Limited edition – 10,000 copies pressed)

That Woman's Got Me Drinking/Her Father Didn't Like Me
Anyway/Roddy McCorley
ZTT Zang 56 T 12″ October 1994

That Woman's Got Me Drinking/Her Father Didn't Like Me
Anyway/Roddy McCorley/Minstrel Boy
ZTT Zang 56 T CD CD October 1994

The Song With No Name/Nancy Whiskey/Cracklin' Rosie
ZTT Zang 60 T 12″ December 1994

The Song With No Name/Nancy Whiskey/Cracklin' Rosie
ZTT Zang 60 T CD CD December 1994

My Way/Song With No Name/Aisling/My Way (Your Way)
ZTT Zang 68 CD CD CD April 1996

Lonesome Highway/A Man Called Horse/Joey's In America
MACG 001 CD CD October 1997

Rock 'N' Roll Paddy/She Moves Through The Fair
MACG OO2 CD CD March 1998

With Nick Cave

What A Wonderful World/A Rainy Night In Soho
Mute 151 D 7″ December 1992

What A Wonderful World/A Rainy Night In Soho/Lucy
Mute 151 12 12″ December 1992

What A Wonderful World/A Rainy Night In Soho/Lucy
Mute 151 CD CD December 1992

With Sinéad O'Connor

Haunted/The Song With No Name/Bring Down The
Lamp/Cracklin' Rosie
ZTT Zang 65 CD CD April 1995

With Marie Brennan

You're The One/Aisling/Victoria
ZTT Zang 68 C CD June 1995

Albums:
(All UK CD releases unless otherwise stated)

The Snake
The Church Of The Holy Spook/Nancy Whiskey/The Song With
No Name/Aisling/Roddy McCorley/Victoria/That Woman's Got
Me Drinking/You're The One/A Mexican Funeral In Paris/
The Rising Of The Moon/The Snake With Eyes Of Garnet/
Haunted/I'll Be Your Handbag/Her Father Didn't Like Me
Anyway/Bring Down The Lamp/Donegal Express
ZTT Zang 4509 98104 2 4 1 CD October 1994
Later re-issued as MACG 004CD CD October 1994

The Crock Of Gold
Paddy Rolling Stone/Rock 'N' Roll Paddy/Paddy Public Enemy
No.1/Back In The County Hell/Lonesome Highway/Come To
The Bower/Céilidh Cowboy/More Pricks Than Kicks/Truck
Drivin' Man/Joey's In America/B&I Ferry/Mother Mo Chroi/
Spanish Lady/St. John Of Gods/Skipping Rhymes/
MacLennan/Wand'rin' Star
ZTT MACG 002 CD November 1997

Siobhan MacGowan

Chariot
Chariot/The Trip/Trust Me/Sin E/Well-Worn Smile/Shoot
Through/Baby/Welcome Child/Celtic Lullaby
Murgatroid MURC D06 CD 1998

Other Appearances/Contributions

Over the past two decades, Shane MacGowan and The Pogues have made a number of guest appearances on various albums, singles and other music related projects. Unfortunately, many of these contributions have now been deleted. What follows, then, are the details of those appearances I have been able to rescue from the vaults of friends, colleagues and the odd reference manual.

Haunted/Junk Theme
The Pogues contributed the above songs (plus 'Hot Dogs With Everything') to the soundtrack of Alex Cox's film *Sid And Nancy – Love Kills*, a stark, yet oddly romantic examination of the doomed love affair between Sex Pistol Sid Vicious and Nancy Spungen. MCA MCG C 6011 LP July 1986. Now deleted.

Dirty Old Town – Live
Live recording of the tune donated by The Pogues to an Irish charity LP – *Live For Ireland*.
MCA 6027 LP 1987. Now deleted.

Kitty – Live
Made available as part of multi-artist single – 'Waves 3' – given away free with *Sounds* in Mid-1988. Now deleted.

Irish Ways
A MacGowan penned/performed song donated to a charity LP entitled *For The Children*.
UK ALIAS ETLP 191 LP 1990. Now deleted.

Miss Otis Regrets/Just One Of Those Things
A Pogues/Kirsty MacColl collaboration recorded for the Aids charity LP *Red, Hot And Blue*.
Chrysalis CHR 1799 LP 1990. Now deleted.

Got A Lot O' Livin' To Do
The Pogues contributed their cover of this song from Elvis Presley's 1957 movie *Loving You* to *The Last Temptation Of Elvis*, a

charity LP benefiting Nordoff Robbins Music Therapy which
featured several artists covering Presley songs, and which was sold
through *New Musical Express.*
Catalogue number unavailable. LP/CD February 1990.
The Pogues also appear on two Various Artists LPs: *Don't Let The
Hope And Anchor Close Down* (released in the mid-Eighties) and
WOMAD's Talking Book – An Introduction To Europe (1987).
Unfortunately, no details are currently available on either release.

Videos

The Pogues

Live At The Town And Country – St. Patrick's Night
Broad Majestic Shannon/If I Should Fall From Grace With God/
Rainy Night In Soho/Thousands Are Sailing/Fairytale Of New
York/Lullaby Of London/Dirty Old Town/London Calling/
Turkish Song Of The Damned/Fiesta/The Irish Rover/
Worms/Rudy, A Message To You/Wild Rover
(Special guests include Kirsty MacColl, Joe Strummer, Lynval
Golding and After Tonight)
VVL Vision Production Films VVD 405 1988 (Running time:
59 minutes)

Completely Pogued
Documentary focusing on The Pogues' career, featuring
contributions from David Byrne and Steve Earle.
Start Productions 1991 (Running time: 55 minutes). Now deleted.

Poguevision
Streams Of Whiskey/Miss Otis Regrets/Just One Of Those
Things/Jack's Heroes/Summer In Siam/White City/A Pair Of
Brown Eyes/Dirty Old Town/Fairytale Of New York/Fiesta/If I
Should Fall From Grace With God/Yeah, Yeah, Yeah, Yeah,
Yeah/Misty Morning, Albert Bridge/A Rainy Night In Soho
Warner Music Vision 9031 75483 3 1991 (Running time:
47 minutes)

5/01 (40397)